WRITING:
A PROJECT-BASED APPROACH

Inspired Project Ideas and Mini-Lessons
to Develop Authentic, Real-World Writing Skills

by Alyssa Eyster, Julie Hussey, and Susan Van Zile

■ SCHOLASTIC

New York • Toronto • London • Auckland
Sydney • New Delhi • Hong Kong

Acknowledgments

To the Great Creator, who generously and lovingly bestows upon us all that we are and all that we have.

To our magnificent students, who inspire us, teach us, and bring us great joy. Thank you for sharing your gifts and talents.

To our families for their abiding love, support, understanding, and encouragement.

To the administration, teachers, parents, and students of the Cumberland Valley School District, who have consistently provided us with a rich and rewarding academic environment in which to grow. We are especially grateful to Patty Hillery for being with us every step of the way.

To Tara Welty, Cameron Gillespie, and Maria L. Chang for making our dreams come true.

To Scholastic for supporting and nurturing children.

Editor: Maria L. Chang
Cover design by Tannaz Fassihi
Cover illustration © Melinda Beck/the iSpot
Interior design by Maria Lilja
Images: p99 © Shutterstock; all other images courtesy of the authors.

ISBN: 978-1-338-46720-8
Scholastic Inc., 557 Broadway, New York, NY 10012
Copyright © 2020 by Alyssa Eyster, Julie Hussey, and Susan Van Zile
Published by Scholastic Inc. All rights reserved.
Printed in the U.S.A.
First printing, January 2020.
1 2 3 4 5 6 7 8 9 10   40   25 24 23 22 21 20

TABLE OF CONTENTS

INTRODUCTION

When Susan was observing a language arts class recently, she heard a student shout, "I hate writing!" Like a searing knife, these words penetrate the hearts of English teachers everywhere. In an era when state assessments require students to write text-dependent analyses (TDAs), and teachers are accountable for test scores, many of us have been so focused on helping students tackle TDAs that we have lost sight of the importance of generating joy and enthusiasm for writing. In our efforts to assist our students and boost their test scores, we have actually reinforced their animosity toward writing.

As classroom teachers who have overemphasized TDA strategies and practices, we collectively decided to revitalize our writing program by investigating project-based learning (PBL) to see how we could incorporate its principles into our language arts curriculum and use them to create exciting, relevant, and meaningful assignments for our students. As we began developing and implementing our PBL units, we were astounded by the results. After analyzing students' responses to the final reflections on the Inventions and Innovations unit (Chapter 6), we saw that 100 percent of the students recommended continuing PBL instruction. They said it is exciting and challenging, requires perseverance and creativity, utilizes technology, and develops communication skills. Their insights and performance during this unit indicate that through PBL, students are acquiring the skills that a National Association of Colleges and Employers survey shows employers value most: the ability to work on a team, solve problems, make decisions, and communicate effectively (Adams, 2014).

Using PBL to Teach Writing

In each unit presented in this book, we incorporate the seven principles of project-based learning and use them as a framework for our lessons, learning activities, and writing assignments. The seven critical design elements of PBL are:

1. a challenging problem or question
2. sustained inquiry
3. authenticity
4. student voice and choice
5. reflection
6. critique and review
7. a public product
   (Larmer, Mergendoller, & Boss, 2015)

Each chapter begins with a driving question that is carried throughout the lessons. We then explain how each of the above elements operates within the unit, since PBL is nonlinear in nature. Although we use PBL principles as a framework, we have modified and adapted them to meet our state standards and to align our instruction and final products to the skills assessed on our school districts' common assessments and benchmarks. (See Core Standards Correlations, pages 8–9.) Rather than having students create a rubric, as PBL proposes, we assess student writing with our districts' grade-level rubrics. Moreover, because our students are just becoming acquainted with project-based learning, we provide planners and guidelines to help them manage their time. In short, our approach to project-based learning accommodates our districts' mandates and limits, but includes more teacher guidance than project-based learning theory advocates.

Given our modifications, how then does our approach differ from traditional approaches to writing? Because the writing is based on students' interests and questions, it becomes meaningful and engaging. Since the process involves inquiry, research, problem-solving, collaboration, and digital writing, students acquire the communication and thinking skills future employers require (Smart, Hicks, & Melton, 2012). Not only does project-based writing prepare students for their future careers, it also fosters the curiosity and enthusiasm that promote lifelong learning.

What's Inside This Book

To develop the instructional units in this book, we used students' ideas and interests to create questions and final products we could connect to the language arts standards, specifically the ones that emphasize writing. For example, when students expressed a desire to create an invention or innovation, we discussed options, and, using student input, generated our driving question: *How do we turn our ideas into inventions and innovations?* From there, we worked backward and decided on our publicly presented products first. Once we knew that students would create a model for an invention/innovation, advertise it using iMovie™, and deliver a multimedia presentation to an authentic audience, we then outlined all of the steps necessary to achieve these goals. Afterward, we aligned each part of the process to the standards.

Each chapter in the book is similarly organized. Since the seven principles of PBL drive the units, we start each one with the PBL framework we used for the instructional design. Lesson plans follow, along with student exemplars and reproducibles, which include planning sheets and rubrics. (All reproducibles are available online at **www.scholastic.com/ pblwriting**. See page 7 for more information on how to access them.) Within each unit we share photos of our work, classroom conversations (where relevant), and examples of our think-alouds and models.

Since PBL involves sustained inquiry, the first unit we teach is research. In **Chapter 1**, we use the topic of "fads" to model the process of conducting research, which includes evaluating sources, taking notes, and creating investigative questions.

In **Chapter 2**, students extend their learning to self-selected topics, conduct research, and design a digital final product that they will publicly share and evaluate. Although these first two units are technically not true project-based learning experiences, they introduce the principles of PBL and give students practice in applying them.

In **Chapter 3**, students examine how to present both sides of a subject to help the public make an informed decision. In this unit, students compare a book with its movie adaptation, read reviews of each, and develop a digital information poster that includes a rating for both the book and the movie and provides pros and cons of each. They then share their final products with another class to help other students make informed decisions about whether to read the book or watch the movie. Since decision-making is a critical skill for project-based learning, students experience the process of making an informed decision as they complete this project.

To prepare students for more extensive project-based learning units, we utilize scaffolding. In **Chapter 4**, students continue to develop their research and technology skills as they investigate nutritious foods, using facts from their research to create an advertisement from the food's point of view. To publicize the ad, students draw a picture of their food and use the web 2.0 tool Blabberize to animate the image and make it talk. Blabberize allows students to record their voices and practice their speaking skills without standing in front of a live audience. We discuss such things as volume and inflection before students record and give them an opportunity to hone these skills. Again, they share final products with other classrooms, and students can vote on their favorites.

In **Chapter 5**, students work in teams to target a specific school-related problem they want to solve. Next, they identify a primary source within the school to help them investigate the problem. Teams then develop interview questions or surveys to gather information about their problems and analyze the results to work toward solutions. To share their explanation of the problems and to offer ideas for solving the problems, students produce a podcast. They share these podcasts with other grade levels, and cross-grade solution teams are formed to work on solving the problem.

Students are now prepared to participate in the Inventions and Innovations unit presented in **Chapter 6**, because they have practiced the skills required to be successful. In this unit, students conceptualize an invention or innovation, conduct surveys to determine its viability, develop and create it, then present it to a panel of judges to convince them to invest in their product.

At the heart of sparking creativity and generating enthusiasm in classrooms is project-based learning. Research demonstrates that instruction emphasizing inquiry and investigation, choice, collaboration, and authentic performance-based assessments increases students' cognitive orientation toward mastery and learning (Blumenfeld et al., 1991; Thomas, 2000). Ironically, in a world where some of us are overemphasizing learning activities and assignments representative of our state tests, studies show that students who receive PBL instruction score higher on standardized and performance-based assessments than students who study similar material using traditional methods (Larmer et al., 2015; Thomas, 2000). Project-based learning activities not only prepare students for the 21st century, they also cultivate curiosity, inspire innovation, and ignite a passion for lifelong learning. If the success of the fifth-grade PBL participants in our classrooms is an indicator, the future looks promising.

References

Adams, S. (2014, November 12). The 10 skills employers want most in 2015. Retrieved April 24, 2017, from *Forbes* at www.forbes.com/sites/susanadams/2014/11/12/the-10-skills-employers-most-want-in-2015-graduates/#5e7a44442511

Blumenfeld, P., Soloway, E., Marx, R., Krajcik, J., Guzdial, M., & Palincsar, A. (1991). Motivating project-based learning: Sustaining the doing, supporting the learning. *Educational Psychologist, 26*(3&4), 369–398.

Larmer, J., Mergendoller, J., & Boss, S. (2015). *Setting the standard for project-based learning: A proven approach to rigorous classroom instruction.* Alexandria, VA: ASCD.

Smart, K. L., Hicks, N., & Melton, J. (2012). Using problem-based scenarios to teach writing. *Business Communication Quarterly, 76*(1), 72–81. doi:10.1177/1080569912466256

Thomas, J. W. (2000). *A review of research on project-based learning.* San Rafael, CA: Autodesk Foundation.

The lessons in this book come with graphic organizers, planners, checklists, rubrics, and more. All of these ready-to-print materials are available online at **www.scholastic.com/pblwriting**. To access them, simply enter your email address and this code: **SC846720**.

INCLUDES
ONLINE
SUPPORT
MATERIALS

Core Standards Correlations

The lessons in this book meet the following core standards.

	Brainstorming, Taking Notes, and Writing With the Class	Researching, Writing, and Publishing Independently	Designing Informational Posters to Compare Books and Movies	Creating Campaigns to Promote Nutritious Foods	Producing Podcasts to Address Schoolwide Issues	Developing, Designing, and Marketing Inventions and Innovations
Writing						
W.1 Write arguments to support claims in an analysis of substantive topics or texts using valid reasoning and relevant and sufficient evidence.			✓	✓	✓	✓
W.2 Write informative/explanatory texts to examine and convey complex ideas and information clearly and accurately through the effective selection, organization, and analysis of content.	✓	✓				
W.4 Produce clear and coherent writing in which the development, organization, and style are appropriate to task, purpose, and audience.	✓	✓	✓	✓	✓	✓
W.5 Develop and strengthen writing as needed by planning, revising, editing, rewriting, or trying a new approach.	✓	✓	✓	✓	✓	✓
W.6 Use technology, including the internet, to produce and publish writing and to interact and collaborate with others.	✓	✓	✓	✓	✓	✓
W.7 Conduct short as well as more sustained research projects based on focused questions, demonstrating understanding of the subject under investigation.	✓	✓	✓	✓	✓	✓
W.8 Gather relevant information from multiple print and digital sources, assess the credibility and accuracy of each source, and integrate the information while avoiding plagiarism.	✓	✓	✓	✓	✓	✓
W.9 Draw evidence from literary or informational texts to support analysis, reflection, and research.	✓	✓	✓	✓	✓	✓
W.10 Write routinely over extended time frames (time for research, reflection, and revision) and shorter time frames (a single sitting or a day or two) for a range of tasks, purposes, and audiences.	✓	✓		✓	✓	✓
Speaking and Listening						
SL.1 Prepare for and participate effectively in a range of conversations and collaborations with diverse partners, building on others' ideas and expressing their own clearly and persuasively.	✓	✓	✓	✓	✓	✓
SL.2 Integrate and evaluate information presented in diverse media and formats, including visually, quantitatively, and orally.		✓	✓	✓	✓	✓

	Brainstorming, Taking Notes, and Writing With the Class	Researching, Writing, and Publishing Independently	Designing Informational Posters to Compare Books and Movies	Creating Campaigns to Promote Nutritious Foods	Producing Podcasts to Address Schoolwide Issues	Developing, Designing, and Marketing Inventions and Innovations
Speaking and Listening (continued)						
SL.4 Present information, findings, and supporting evidence such that listeners can follow the line of reasoning and the organization, development, and style are appropriate to task, purpose, and audience.	✓	✓	✓	✓	✓	✓
SL.5 Make strategic use of digital media and visual displays of data to express information and enhance understanding of presentations.	✓	✓	✓	✓	✓	✓
SL.6 Adapt speech to a variety of contexts and communicative tasks, demonstrating command of formal English when indicated or appropriate.		✓		✓	✓	✓
Reading: Informational Text						
RI.5.7 Draw on information from multiple print or digital resources, demonstrating the ability to locate an answer to a question quickly or to solve a problem efficiently.	✓	✓	✓	✓	✓	✓
RI.5.9 Integrate information from several texts on the same topic in order to write or speak about the subject knowledgeably.	✓	✓	✓	✓	✓	
Language						
L.1 Demonstrate command of the conventions of standard English grammar and usage when writing or speaking.	✓	✓	✓	✓	✓	✓
L.2 Demonstrate command of the conventions of standard English capitalization, punctuation, and spelling when writing.	✓	✓	✓	✓	✓	✓
L.5.3 Use knowledge of language and its conventions when writing, speaking, reading, or listening.	✓	✓	✓	✓	✓	✓
L.5.6 Acquire and use accurately grade-appropriate general academic and domain-specific words and phrases, including those that signal contrast, addition, and other logical relationships (e.g., *however, although, nevertheless, similarly, moreover, in addition*).	✓	✓	✓	✓	✓	✓

BRAINSTORMING, TAKING NOTES, AND WRITING WITH THE CLASS

CHAPTER 1

The first two chapters of this book prepare students for project-based learning by guiding them through the process of conducting research, taking notes, writing an essay, and other steps in between.

For this unit, we use the topic of "fads" to model the research and writing process. We provide a couple of articles to get you started, but you may want to supply students with more articles to allow them to concentrate on drawing information from multiple texts. Since learning how to take notes and use them to craft a piece of writing are difficult skills, we deliberately scaffolded the research process as we modeled it.

In this unit, students write a five-paragraph research essay. However, feel free to adapt and modify this writing assignment.

Project-Based Learning Framework

Challenging Problem or Question

Inquiry and investigation form the foundation of project-based learning (PBL). Consequently, knowing how to conduct research is essential. To set the purpose for learning, students investigate this driving question: *How do we investigate and write about a topic?* As students engage in the process of answering this question, they participate in meaningful learning activities designed to introduce them to and deepen their understanding of the research and writing process. Starting here helps students acquire the research skills that are an integral part of project-based learning.

Sustained Inquiry

Students brainstorm what they already know about conducting research, then generate a series of questions to help them acquire the knowledge they need to answer the driving question (Larmer, Mergendoller, & Boss, 2015). Questions include the following:

- How do we assess what we already know about a topic?
- How do we take notes?
- How can peers provide feedback to improve note-taking skills?

- How do we use notes from different sources to write paragraphs?
- How do we revise and edit our writing?
- How do we develop a thesis statement?
- How do we create hooks and introductions?
- How do we conclude a piece of writing?

Authenticity

The context of this project is authentic, because students learn how to effectively take and evaluate notes and conduct research to write about a topic under investigation. Student researchers use Google Docs to write a five-paragraph essay about fads.

Student Voice and Choice

Encourage students to come up with their own way to research the topic of "fads," writing individual goals in their writer's notebooks. Later, they use their voices to comment on classmates' notes and share their ideas on what makes a good piece of writing.

Reflection

Metacognition plays an important role in learning, because being aware of the processes and strategies involved in acquiring knowledge helps deepen students' understanding and ability to apply these skills in other contexts (Fadel, Trilling, & Bialik, 2015). Because we want students to use their research skills in future units, ask them to reflect on the process with prompts such as:

- Use pictures, words, or both to describe your research process.
- Share your process with a partner.
- Discuss similarities and differences you observe.

In addition, partners interview each other about evaluating sources, and students reflect on their revisions to expand their repertoire of revision strategies and set goals for future revision. Although the format of students' reflections may differ, they reflect to solidify their understanding of the research and writing process.

Critique and Revision

Through the process of learning how to investigate and write about ideas, students critique and revise their own and others' notes, learn how to use the information to build body paragraphs, and edit and revise thesis statements, introductions, body paragraphs, and conclusions. When students craft paragraphs about their topics, they engage in peer revision and editing and conference with the teacher when necessary.

Public Products

Students produce a five-paragraph essay about fads, along with notes and shorter pieces of writing, that they share with classmates and their teacher.

Reference

Fadel, C., Trilling, B., & Bialik, M. (2015). *Four-dimensional education: The competencies learners need to succeed*. Boston, MA: Create Space Independent Publishing Platform.

LESSON 1: Brainstorming What We Know

Estimated Teaching Time: One 45-minute class period

Before You Start: Make a Pocket Research Organizer to serve as a model: Fold the short side of a 12-by-18-inch sheet of construction paper to about half an inch from the top. Use a long-reach stapler to create three pockets, stapling them 6 inches apart.

Materials
- copy paper for each student
- 12-by-18-inch construction paper for each student
- long-reach stapler
- scissors

Driving Question: How do we investigate and write about a topic?

Critical Question: How do we assess what we already know about a topic?

Warm-Up: As a class, discuss what a "fad" is and

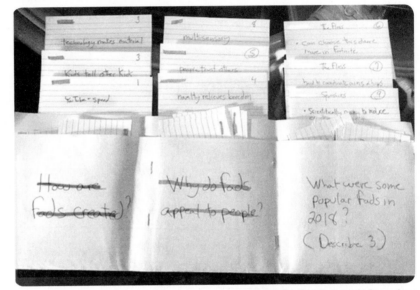

Sample Pocket Research Organizer

list students' responses on the whiteboard. Then talk about some recent fads, why they started, and why they appeal to people. Write the following research questions on the board:

- How are fads created?
- Why do fads appeal to people?
- What were some popular fads from last year? (Describe three.)

Teaching Steps

1. Direct students to fold a sheet of copy paper into eight sections. In each square, have them write one fact or idea related to each of the research questions above. Tell them to use words and phrases, not complete sentences, and to use more paper if necessary.

2. Distribute construction paper to students and model how to make a Pocket Research Organizer (see Before You Start). Have students write one research question on each pocket.

3. Tell students to cut up their notes and place each one into the appropriate organizer pocket. Have students discard notes that do not relate to any of the questions.

Wrap-Up: Pair up students and have them take turns sharing what they already know about the three research questions.

LESSON 2: Taking Notes

Estimated Teaching Time: One 45-minute class period

Before You Start: Collect some articles on fads for the class to use. (We provide two articles with the online resources; see page 7.) Number each article in the upper right-hand corner, so that the first article you'll use to model note-taking is labeled "1."

Prior to starting the lesson, distribute the following materials to students.

- quart-size plastic bags
- lined index cards
- 3 different-color highlighters for each student
- red and blue pens

Have students place the index cards, highlighters, and pens in the plastic bag to make Research Tool Kits. Then have them fold their Pocket Research Organizers (from Lesson 1) into thirds and place them in their bags. Tell students to store all their research materials in their Research Tool Kits for the remainder of the unit.

Materials
- copies of "Fad Frenzy" article from *Scholastic Math* (Reproducible 1A)
- copies of "Toy Craze" article from *Scholastic News* (Reproducible 1B)
- students' Research Tool Kits (see Before You Start)
- writer's notebooks
- articles on fads
- classroom projection system

Driving Question: How do we investigate and write about a topic?

Critical Question: How do we take notes?

Warm-Up: In their writer's notebooks, ask students to jot down what they know about note-taking. As a class, decide on a universal acronym for note-taking, like the one below. Post it in the classroom and have students write it on the back of their Pocket Research Organizer.

- **N** – needs to be own words
- **O** – organized
- **T** – topic-related
- **E** – each card has one fact
- **S** – short phrases

TIP As you decide which articles to use for whole-group instruction, remember to scaffold. To begin, choose articles that primarily address the first question. Gradually, add articles that include answers to all three research questions. Another approach is to read an article three times, searching for answers to one question at a time.

(Available online; see page 7.)

Acronym to help students remember how to take notes

Teaching Steps

1. Direct students to take out their Research Tool Kits. Distribute article #1. Tell students to write the source number and the title of the article on the back of their Pocket Research Organizer.

2. As a class, use three different-color highlighters to color-code the research questions on the front of the Pocket Research Organizer.

3. On the whiteboard, display a copy of article #1 for the class to see. Read aloud the article and highlight the information that addresses one of the questions in the appropriate color.

4. After highlighting, model how to take notes on an index card: Color-code the card in the upper left-hand corner. Put the source number in the upper right-hand corner. Paraphrase the information. Use the NOTES acronym to write the notes. Place the index card in the appropriate pocket of your Pocket Research Organizer.

> **TIP** Having students keep a record of the articles they use for research emphasizes the importance of citing sources to avoid plagiarism and serves as a preview to our lesson on citing sources (page 36). It also helps students see the importance of cross-checking facts across multiple sources.

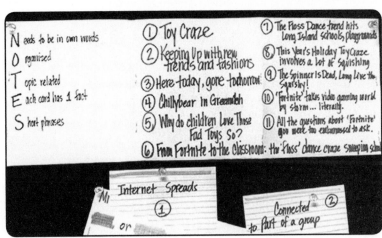

Sources numbered and listed on the back of Pocket Research Organizer

5. As you continue reading the article, thinking aloud, and taking notes, begin to involve the class in the process. Ask students to raise their hands when they hear an answer to one of the research questions. Call on individuals to paraphrase the information they identified. Demonstrate how to quickly skim information that does not relate to the research question.

6. When the class appears to understand the process, pair up students and have them choose an article for note-taking. Ask partners to read through the article together and take notes. Record your observations about student progress. Monitor and adjust instruction accordingly.

Wrap-Up: Pair up students and have them critique each other's note cards. Instruct them to discard notes that do not relate to the topic or follow the rules of the NOTES acronym.

> **TIP** As we monitored partners during this phase of instruction, we observed two common mistakes: notes written in sentences and notes containing irrelevant information. To address these issues, we collected some of the sentences and asked the class to shorten them into phrases. Next, we used a volunteer's note cards to model how to identify irrelevant information. Each time we read a note, we showed how it related to the question. For example, if a card that says "word of mouth" appears in the pocket asking "How are fads created?" we simply state that this card shows fads spread because people talk to one another; it relates to the question. However, if a card reads "ban on fidget spinners," we remark that banning a fad does not relate to how fads are created, so it doesn't belong in that pocket.

LESSON 3: Individual Note-Taking

Estimated Teaching Time: One 45-minute class period, plus a week of centers

Materials
- students' Research Tool Kits
- writer's notebooks
- articles on fads in pocket folders

Driving Question: How do we investigate and write about a topic?

Critical Question: How do we evaluate and refine our notes?

Warm-Up: Direct students to take out their Research Tool Kits and reread their notes. Ask them to create a goal for improving their note-taking skills. Use the acronym NOTES to model a few examples of attainable goals such as: "Use my own words or phrases instead of copying the sentence from the text," or "Make sure my notes answer my research questions." Then, have students write their individual goals in their writer's notebooks.

Teaching Steps

1. Place pocket folders with numbered articles in a central location where students can access.

2. Pair up students. (Today's partners will collaborate to write the second body paragraph in Lesson 5.) Tell students to choose a minimum of three articles to read and use to take notes.

3. Instruct students to write their notes individually even though they are reading the same articles with their partners. Circulate through the room and conference with students as they take notes.

Copies of articles for students to take

Wrap-Up: Ask students to reread the goal they set in the Warm-Up. In their writer's notebooks, have them explain how they met their goals. If they did not meet their goals, direct students to develop an action plan to attain them.

LESSON 4: Evaluating Notes

Estimated Teaching Time: One 45-minute class period

Materials
- writer's notebooks
- students' Research Tool Kits
- copies of Peer Review for Note-Taking (Reproducible 1C)
- sticky notes

Driving Question: How do we investigate and write about a topic?

Critical Question: How can peers provide feedback to improve note-taking skills?

Warm-Up: In their writer's notebooks, have students answer this question: *What is constructive criticism?* Pair up students and ask them to share their responses. As a class, have students offer both examples and non-examples of constructive criticism. Write these in two separate columns on the board. Discuss language that an observer might hear when listening to productive peer conferences.

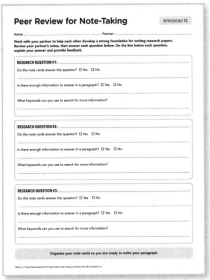

(Available online; see page 7.)

Examples of Constructive Criticism	Non-Examples of Constructive Criticism
I think you need more information about how fads get started because you have only one idea.	You don't have enough information.
Have you considered narrowing your search from "video games" to "Fortnite"?	You need to search using other keywords.

Teaching Steps

1. Pass out copies of Peer Review for Note-Taking.

2. Ask a student volunteer to bring the handout and his or her Pocket Research Organizer to the front of the class. Spread out the note cards from pocket 3 ("What were some popular fads from last year?"). Model how to use the Peer Review sheet to provide constructive feedback designed to help the student improve.

3. Pair up students and have them use the forms to evaluate each other's notes.

Wrap-Up: On a sticky note, ask students to write down one thing they learned from their partner that will help them improve their note-taking skills. Collect these and post them on chart paper with the title "How to Improve Note-Taking Skills."

LESSON 5: Turning Notes Into Body Paragraphs

Estimated Teaching Time: Three 45-minute class periods

Materials
- note cards from pocket 1 of teacher's Pocket Research Organizer (from Lesson 2)
- classroom projection system
- computers or tablets with internet access
- access to Google Docs

Driving Question: How do we investigate and write about a topic?

Critical Question: How do we use notes from different sources to write paragraphs?

Warm-Up: Pair up students and have partners take turns telling each other the characteristics of a well-written paragraph. Then, invite partners to share their ideas with the class.

Teaching Steps

1. Display your note cards from pocket 1 ("How are fads created?") on the board. Think aloud to show students how to group similar ideas together and how to arrange these groups in a logical order. (See Teacher Model, page 18.)

2. Show students how to turn the research question into a topic sentence. Type the sentence into a Google Doc, which you will share with students.

3. Demonstrate how to use the note cards to write supporting details. Talk about how to use transition words to connect one idea to another. At the end of the paragraph, model how to create a clincher sentence that sums up the main idea and transitions into the next body paragraph. Tell students that the transition between paragraphs can also be included in the topic sentence of the next paragraph. Show them how to do both.

4. After modeling how to draft the first body paragraph, pair up students with their note-taking partners. Have them work together to use this process to draft body paragraph two, which addresses the second research question. Have them type their paragraph into a shared Google Doc. Be available to help students as they work through the process.

5. Once partners have completed their second body paragraph, direct students to write the third body paragraph individually.

Wrap-Up: Have students share their third body paragraphs with their partner. Instruct them to compare their paragraphs. Ask them to suggest one change their partner can make to his or her writing.

> **TIP** On Google Docs, make a copy of the model first paragraph, title it with the student partners' names, and then share it with each pair. For example, say Tomás and Natalia are partners. Make a copy of the model paragraph, name the document "Tomás and Natalia," and share it with them. After they have written their second paragraph together, make a copy of that document to share with each student in the pair. This way, Tomás and Natalia each have a copy of the document in which to add his or her own third paragraph.

The processes and skills students acquire and use continuously during PBL transfer to other content. For example, when students address a TDA question, they close-read multiple texts to find evidence to answer the question. This is exactly what students do in this lesson—they highlight their evidence, take notes, and organize their notes into sentences and paragraphs. Help students see the similarities and connect their prior knowledge to the new content.

Teacher Model

As I look at my notes and think about the topic of my paragraph, how fads are created, I see that three of my note cards—"the internet," "YouTube," and "social media"—relate to fads being spread through technology, so I will group these ideas together. I also see that "celebrities" and "the desire to imitate them" relate, so I will pair them. Two cards show fads originate through word of mouth, and three cards show toy developers use catchy ads and cheaper technology to produce new products that jump-start fads. I'll make two more groups, then.

Now that I have grouped my note cards, I can use my research question to help me write my topic sentence. I can turn the question into a statement: *Fads are created. . .* How can I finish this? I notice that as different as fads are, they start in similar ways, so I can say: *Fads are created in similar ways.* Boring! What can I do to jazz this up? Hmmm. I'll try alliteration. How is this? *From Fortnite to the Floss, fads start in similar ways.* I like that topic sentence.

Next, I will use my note cards to create the supporting details. Since the internet, YouTube, and social media cause fads, I'll start with those. I can say: *Because of the internet, YouTube, and social media, fads spread like wildfire across the world.* I like the simile and hyperbole there. Now, I need to think about what to write next.

Another way fads spread quickly is when celebrities start them, so I can write: *When a celebrity whom people want to imitate endorses a fad, it catches on even faster.*

I'm stuck. How do I connect the idea of fads spread by word of mouth to fads spread through technology and celebrities? Maybe I can say: *Technology and celebrities are not the only ways fads ignite.* Yes, that will do it. My next sentence can be: *Sometimes a new craze begins when kids tell other kids about it.* I don't need

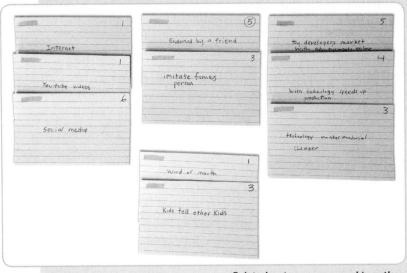

Related notes are grouped together.

to say "word of mouth," which is on my other note card, because that just repeats what I wrote.

I'm stumped again. How do I connect the idea that toy developers use fast, cheap technology to market glitzy new toys to how fads are created? Let's see . . . Since kids constantly want new stuff, toy developers make inexpensive new products to meet kids' needs. Kids rush out to buy these new toys, which starts a fad. How can I put these ideas into a sentence that fits with the others? I'll try this: *Since the younger generation craves new products, toy developers use new technology to produce glitzy, cheap items kids rush to buy.* Whoa! That's a mouthful, but it makes sense. I can revise it later. Uh-oh! I need to connect this sentence back to my topic. How can I do that? I might need to add a sentence like this: *Within a short time, the toy becomes a new fad.*

I've used all my note cards now. What can I do to wrap up the paragraph? This is tough, because I want to sum up what I've said and lead the reader into my next paragraph about why fads appeal to people. What I've said here is that fads start in similar ways. But I know from my research that fads appeal to people for different reasons. I need to put those two ideas together. I'll try this: *Even though fads have common origins, they attract people for different reasons.* Phew, I think that will work. I can always change it later. At least it is different from my topic sentence and does its job.

Below is the draft of body paragraph one based on the think-aloud.

Teacher Model of Body Paragraph One

From Fortnite to the Floss, fads start in similar ways. Because of the internet, YouTube, and social media, fads spread like wildfire across the world. When a celebrity whom people want to imitate endorses a fad, it catches on even faster. Technology and celebrities are not the only ways fads ignite. Sometimes a new craze begins when kids tell other kids about it. Since the younger generation craves new products, toy developers use new technology to produce glitzy, cheap items kids rush to buy. Within a short time, the toy becomes a fad. Even though fads have common origins, they attract people for different reasons.

LESSON 6: Revising Body Paragraphs

Estimated Teaching Time: One 45-minute class period

Before You Start: Prior to teaching this lesson, read students' paragraphs from Lesson 5. (We have our students save them on our Google Drive.) Select three paragraphs, including the teacher model you generated, for students to revise. Ask each writer's permission to share his or her work anonymously. Then copy and paste these paragraphs, beginning with yours, into a single document to project onto the whiteboard and print copies for students.

Materials
- copies of sample paragraphs to revise (see Before You Start)
- classroom projection system
- red pens
- writer's notebooks

Driving Question: How do we investigate and write about a topic?

Critical Question: How do we revise our writing?

Warm-Up: Teach or review the revision strategy ARMS—add, remove, move, and substitute—and the proofreading symbols associated with each strategy. Create an anchor chart (see photo at right) for the acronym and invite students to suggest specific ideas associated with each strategy. For example, a writer could add vivid verbs, similes, and sensory language. As the year progresses, add more ideas to the chart.

Teaching Steps

1. Distribute copies of the sample paragraphs for students to revise (see Before You Start).

2. Display the first body paragraph—the teacher model from the previous lesson— on the whiteboard.

3. Use think-aloud to model how to revise the paragraph. Emphasize which of the ARMS strategies you are applying to the writing.

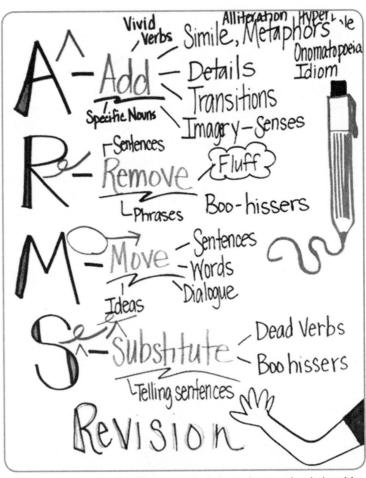

ARMS acronym to help students revise their writing

4. Pair up students and have partners revise the second paragraph together.

5. Have students revise the third paragraph individually.

6. Direct students to reread all three of their revised paragraphs and make additional revisions if necessary.

Wrap-Up: Have students look at their revisions and respond to the following questions in their writer's notebooks: *What are two revision strategies you used? What is one revision strategy you need to use in the future?*

Below is an example of a revision our class did together.

Student Paragraph Before Revision

Fads can appeal to people for many reasons. Fads can make people fit in or be a part of a group. In addition, people can be taught skill while playing with there new popular fads, like Rubix cubes. These toys can give people something to touch. It is also an outlet (something to do), other than electronic devices. Some fads can give you a brain break or relieve stress. Toys like squishies can do this. These are some of the many ways that fads appeal to people.

Student Paragraph After Class Revision

Most kids eat, sleep, and breathe fads because of their appealing nature. People want to be involved in the next latest craze to be a part of the crowd. In addition, people can be taught skills, such as algorithms and problem-solving, while playing with their new popular toys like Rubix cubes. These hands-on toys can give people something to touch instead of relying on their daily use of electronic devices. On the other hand, some fads can give kids a brain break from everyday routines or relieve stress. Toys like squishies can do this. Due to their novelty, fads appeal to people because they build skills, relieve stress, and stimulate the senses.

Note: When revising as a class, it is difficult to correct new problems we create. For example, the third sentence is awkward and wordy. Therefore, we have students reread their revisions and make additional changes.

TIP Clinchers are often difficult for students to write. One strategy is to have students list the main points of the paragraph in the margin. Then have them look at the list and try to craft a sentence summarizing their main points.

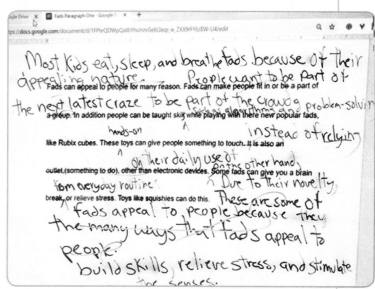

Revisions suggested by the class

LESSON 7: Editing

Estimated Teaching Time: One 45-minute class period

Before You Start: Prior to teaching this lesson, choose three student paragraphs from Lesson 5 for the class to edit. If possible, pick one with a run-on sentence. Ask each writer's permission to share his or her work anonymously. Then copy and paste these paragraphs into a single document to project onto the whiteboard and print copies for students.

Materials
- copies of sample paragraphs to edit (see Before You Start)
- classroom projection system
- blue pens
- students' own paragraphs (from Lesson 6)
- writer's notebooks

Driving Question: How do we investigate and write about a topic?

Critical Question: How do we edit our writing?

Warm-Up: On the whiteboard, display a student's run-on sentence that also contains other errors. Pair up students and have them identify the errors and discuss how to correct them. Call on volunteers to come to the whiteboard to correct the errors, reminding them to use proper proofreading symbols. Introduce the acronym CUPS (capitalization, usage, punctuation, spelling) to help students remember what editors check. Review any proofreading symbols that were not used in the model sentence.

Teaching Steps

1. Distribute copies of the sample paragraphs for students to edit (see Before You Start).

2. Display the first sample paragraph on the whiteboard and ask the class to suggest edits. Using blue pens, have students use proofreading symbols to mark up their copies of the paragraph as you make the changes on the whiteboard.

3. Pair up students and have partners edit the second paragraph together.

4. Have students edit the third paragraph individually.

5. Review students' edits as a class.

6. Direct students to edit their own drafts.

Wrap-Up: Display the following sentences:

> A. Let's eat, Mike.
> B. Lets eat Mike.

> **TIP** If students are editing their drafts on Google Docs, consider doing a lesson to show students how to use the Review menu to edit.

Discuss what causes the different meanings of the sentences. In their writer's notebooks, have students write a few sentences about why editing is important. Also, ask them to generate two sentences in which editing makes a difference.

LESSON 8: Developing a Thesis Statement

Estimated Teaching Time: One 45-minute class period

Before You Start: Print a copy of Model Student Introductions (Reproducible 1D). Cut the paragraphs apart and enlarge each paragraph. Display the paragraphs around the room.

Materials
- copy of Model Student Introductions (Reproducible 1D)
- pencils, paper, highlighters
- copies of What Is a Thesis Statement? (Reproducible 1E)
- copies of Thesis Statement Framework (Reproducible 1F)

Driving Question: How do we investigate and write about a topic?

Critical Question: How do we develop a thesis statement?

Warm-Up: Announce to the class that you posted a few introductions to research papers around the room. Invite students to go on a gallery tour of the introductions. Send a group of three or four students, armed with pencils and paper, to each paragraph. Direct students to read the introduction to identify its characteristics and to list them on their paper. When students finish reading their first introduction, rotate them through the remaining ones. As a class, discuss what students have noticed about the introductions and record their observations on chart paper. Responses should indicate that an introduction includes a hook, a sentence or two of background information about the topic, and a main-idea statement (thesis).

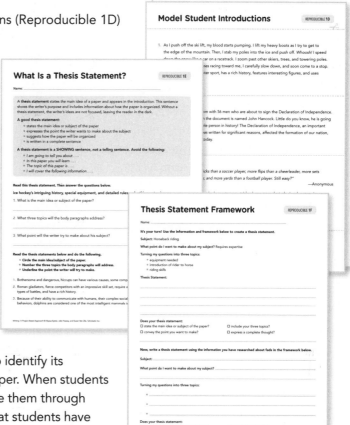

(Available online; see page 7.)

Afterward, send students on a second gallery tour, instructing them to find the sentence in each introduction that tells the main idea of the paper. Then, ask volunteers to come up and point to the sentence stating the main idea and read it aloud. After reading each thesis statement, ask students what the subject (main idea) of the paper is and what three pieces of information the writer will include in the body of the paper. For example, if the thesis statement is "With their fascinating history, rapid evolution, and promising future, movies are guaranteed to keep changing," the subject is "movies." In the body of the paper, the writer will discuss movies' history, evolution, and future. Finally, ask: *What point will the writer try to make about movies? What will he emphasize in the paper?* Lead students to discover the writer's point: *Movies change constantly.* Tell students that the sentences they identified are called "thesis statements." Pair up students and ask them to come up with a definition for "thesis statement" and to share it with the class.

Teaching Steps

1. Distribute copies of What Is a Thesis Statement? Read the definition of a thesis statement and have students highlight the keywords. Compare this definition to theirs. Review what makes a good thesis statement.

2. With students, read the boldface thesis statement on the handout: *Ice hockey's intriguing history, special equipment, and detailed rules make this sport unique.* As a class, identify and circle the subject or main idea (*ice hockey*). Number the three pieces of information the writer will talk about in the body (*history, equipment, and rules*). Underline the point the writer will emphasize (*these things make the sport unique*).

3. Ask partners to work together to mark up the first thesis sentence in the bottom part of the handout. Then have students mark up the other two sentences independently. Review their answers.

4. Pass out copies of the Thesis Statement Framework. Ask partners to use the information in the first section to create a thesis statement—for example, "Horseback riding requires expertise in the equipment, introducing the rider to the horse, and riding skills."

5. After students share their thesis statements, ask them to create one for fads (the topic of their research).

Students reviewing introductions

Wrap-Up: Pair up students. Have them exchange their thesis statements and circle the main idea, number the three topics, and underline the writer's point. Tell them to make sure the sentence makes sense. If it does not, have students revise it. Collect students' thesis statements and use them for formative assessment. Adjust the next lesson based on what you observe. For example, if students have difficulty creating the three points, show several examples of the sentences containing this problem and revise them as a class.

LESSON 9: Writing the Introduction

Estimated Teaching Time: One 45-minute class period

Materials
- enlarged, cutout copies of Model Student Introductions (from Lesson 8)
- copies of Introductions and Hooks (Reproducible 1G)
- copies of Brainstorming Hooks (Reproducible 1H)
- students' thesis statements (from Lesson 8)
- classroom projection system

Driving Question: How do we investigate and write about a topic?

Critical Question: How do we create hooks and introductions?

Warm-Up: Revisit the model introductions from Lesson 8 and focus on the hooks. Read each hook (the first sentence) one at a time and ask students what each does to grab the reader's attention. Elicit responses, such as: uses a quotation, asks a question, tells a story, talks directly to the reader, employs vivid description.

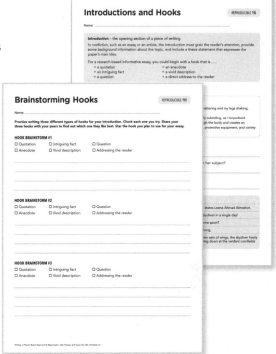

(Available online; see page 7.)

Teaching Steps

1. Distribute copies of Introductions and Hooks. Read the definition for *introduction*, and have students highlight the three characteristics of an introduction.

2. Review the types of hooks in the bulleted list. Ask students to identify the type of hook used in each of the model introductions displayed around the room.

3. Read the model introduction on the handout and answer the three questions about it as a class. (*Answers: 1. Anecdote 2. Thesis statement: Because of its unique history, protective equipment, and variety of competitions, skydiving proves to be an exhilarating extreme sport. The writer's point is that skydiving is an exhilarating extreme sport.*) Have students mark up the thesis statement on their copies by circling the subject or main idea, numbering the three topics, and underlining the writer's point.

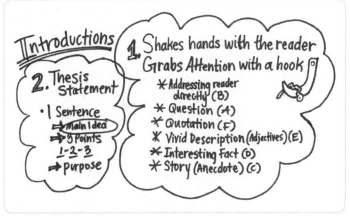

Anchor chart showing characteristics of an introduction

4. Review the other hooks the writer could have used. Note that hooks that directly address the reader may include the pronouns *you* or *your*.

5. Pass out copies of Brainstorming Hooks. Direct students to write three different hooks for the introduction to their fads research paper.

6. Pair up students and have them share their three hooks. After discussing their work, tell students to circle the hook they will use to begin their introduction.

7. Return students' thesis statements from the previous lesson. On the whiteboard, share examples of students' statements that represent common problems you observed from reading them. Demonstrate how to correct those problems, and have students reexamine their thesis statements and rewrite them, if necessary.

8. Model how to construct the introduction, including how to use transition sentence(s) to connect the hook to the thesis statement. (See Teacher Model below.)

9. Direct students to use their hooks and thesis statements to write their introductions. Encourage them to revisit the introductions hanging around the room to see additional examples of transition sentences.

Wrap-Up: Pair up students and tell partners to number themselves 1 and 2. As partner 1 reads his or her introduction, partner 2 does the following:

- forms a hook in the air to identify the hook
- links fingers when he or she hears a transition
- makes a T-shape with the hands when the thesis statement is stated, and then raises one finger each time one of the three topics is read
- shares compliments and suggests improvements

Have students switch roles and repeat this process before making revisions.

Teacher Model

I already have the hook I am going to use to start my introduction: *Remember big hair, monster balls, and the Walkman? Of course not!* I have also written my thesis statement: *Fleeting fads quickly come and go, but they originate in similar ways, appeal to people, and enjoy momentary popularity.* Now, how do I create sentences that connect my hook to my thesis statement?

My hook mentions fads that few kids today will remember because those fads disappeared. My thesis statement emphasizes the idea that fads do not last long. Therefore, the sentences I use to connect the two should relate to the idea that fads are short-lived. Maybe my next sentence can be: *The reason no one remembers these former fads is that they disappeared almost instantly.* The sentence makes sense here, but I want to add pop and include some figurative language. What's something that does not last very long—a hiccup, a sneeze, a bubble? I think I'll say: *These former fads lasted about as long as a sneeze.* That's better. I have some alliteration and a comparison. I want to add another sentence that reinforces the temporary nature of fads before I transition into my thesis statement. One thing I learned is that trends are different from fads because a trend lasts longer. Perhaps I can say something like this: *Unlike trends, fads catch on instantly and then fade.* I like that contrast. To connect my thesis statement to this sentence, I need to change it slightly. I think I will add the transition word *although*. I might have to change my wording slightly to have the sentence make sense. I'll try: *Although fleeting fads come and go quickly, they originate in similar ways, appeal to people, and enjoy momentary popularity*. That sounds better than my original thesis statement and seems to make more sense.

Below is the draft of the introduction based on the think-aloud.

Teacher Example of Introduction

Remember big hair, monster balls, and the Walkman? Of course not! These former fads lasted about as long as a sneeze. Unlike trends, fads catch on instantly and then fade. Although fleeting fads come and go quickly, they originate in similar ways, appeal to people, and enjoy momentary popularity.

LESSON 10: Writing the Conclusion

Estimated Teaching Time: One 45-minute class period

Materials
- copies of Sample Conclusions (Reproducible 1I)
- copies of Brainstorming Conclusions (Reproducible 1J)
- chart paper

Driving Question: How do we investigate and write about a topic?

Critical Question: How do we conclude a piece of writing?

Warm-Up: Have students write a draft of their conclusion. Divide the class into two equal groups and have them form two concentric circles—an inner and an outer one—with students facing each other. Direct students in the outer circle to share their conclusions with their partners in the inner circle. Then have students in the inner circle take a turn sharing their conclusions. Afterward, have members of the outer circle move clockwise to the next person and repeat the sharing process. After students have heard three or four conclusions, have them sit down and nominate classmates who wrote strong conclusions. Ask these students to read their conclusions aloud, while the rest of the class thinks about what makes each conclusion effective.

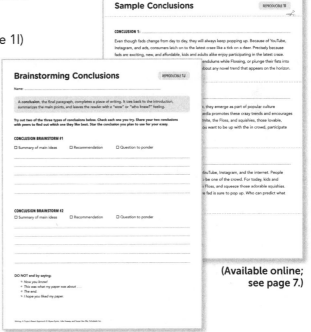

(Available online; see page 7.)

Teaching Steps

1. With the class, create an anchor chart that defines *conclusion* and lists some of its common characteristics. Also, discuss and record on the chart what conclusions should not do. For example, note that conclusions should not end by saying:

   - "Now you know . . ."
   - "This was what my paper was about."
   - "The end."
   - "I hope you liked my paper."

2. Distribute copies of Sample Conclusions. Have students read the first conclusion and then ask them what they notice about it. Lead students to observe that this conclusion starts with a sentence that restates the main idea and/or emphasizes the point the writer makes about the subject. The sentences that follow sum up the topic of each body paragraph. Finally, the writer ends with a final thought about the subject. Have students label this conclusion "Summary of Main Ideas."

3. Next, read the second conclusion and ask students to compare it to the first one. What similarities and differences do they notice? Have students underline the final sentence of this paragraph and ask them what they observe. (*It makes a recommendation and directly addresses the reader.*) Tell students to label this conclusion "Recommendation." Follow the same process for the third conclusion, noting that this one ends with a question to ponder. Direct students to label the paragraph "Question to Ponder."

4. Distribute copies of Brainstorming Conclusions. Invite them to practice writing two of the three types of conclusions. Remind them to refer to the conclusion they wrote during the Warm-Up to see if they can incorporate any of the information into their new conclusions.

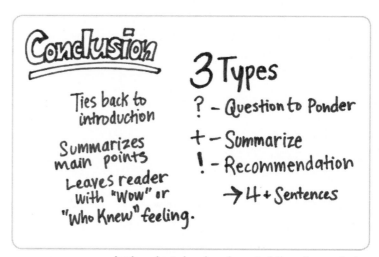

Anchor chart showing characteristics of a conclusion

Wrap-Up: Ask for volunteers to read aloud their conclusions. Have the class decide if it is a summary, a recommendation, or a question to ponder. Ask students to provide evidence for their choices.

Note: After this lesson, have students type their introductions and conclusions into the Google Docs containing their three body paragraphs. Since much of what we do with the fads research is introduce and practice skills students need to research and write about a topic, we evaluate their writing for completion. (If you want, you could create a rubric that assesses the introduction, body paragraph three, and the conclusion, since we wrote body paragraph one as a class and body paragraph two with a partner.) This unit serves as a building block for the next chapter.

RESEARCHING, WRITING, AND PUBLISHING INDEPENDENTLY

CHAPTER 2

Having gained experience researching and writing collaboratively about a class topic (fads) in Chapter 1, students are now ready to practice these skills with a topic they choose for themselves. They formulate their own research questions, evaluate sources, take notes from websites and articles they find themselves, and write a five-paragraph essay. As they go through this process, they review some of the lessons from the previous chapter. Finally, they publish their essay using the app Book Creator and present it to an audience.

Project-Based Learning Framework

Challenging Problem or Question

In this unit, students select a topic they're interested in and apply what they've learned about the research and writing process to produce a digital book about it. To set the purpose for learning, students investigate this driving question: *How do we research and write about a topic of our choice and share our learning with others?* As students engage in the process of answering this question, they participate in meaningful learning activities designed to deepen their understanding of the research and writing process and how to present a topic to others for critique.

Sustained Inquiry

The following questions are designed to help students acquire the knowledge they need to answer the driving question.

- How do we choose a topic to research?
- How do we generate research questions to investigate a topic?
- How do we evaluate sources for authenticity and reliability?
- How do we cite sources?
- How do we revise and organize notes to write paragraphs?
- How do we write a thesis statement and introduction?
- How do we craft a meaningful conclusion?
- How do we revise and edit our writing?
- How do we use technology to publish information about a topic and share it with others?

Authenticity

The context of this project is authentic because student researchers produce digital books using the Book Creator app and share them with other classes. As students view and listen to each presentation on iPads or tablets, they not only learn about the various topics, but they also use an evaluation sheet to assess each project.

Student Voice and Choice

Individual students have complete autonomy over the topic they choose to research. Before students select their own topic of interest, they investigate a wide range of subjects. A passionate cat lover, for example, may investigate the role cats played in Egyptian culture, while another student may research the Battle of the Bulge. Within the Book Creator app, students choose the formatting, visuals, and videos they want to incorporate.

Reflection

Metacognition plays an important role in learning, because being aware of the processes and strategies involved in acquiring knowledge helps deepen students' understanding and ability to apply these skills in other contexts (Fadel, Trilling, & Bialik, 2015). Student partners interview each other about evaluating sources, and individuals reflect on their revisions to expand their repertoire of strategies. Although students use different formats to reflect on their work, they consistently use reflection to solidify their understanding of the research and writing process.

Critique and Revision

To help students narrow down their topics and create their three research questions, they conference individually and in small groups with their peers and teacher. As they select their sources, students use a checklist to evaluate each one for the 3Rs: reliability, recency, and relevance. After taking notes, peers critique one another's note cards to determine whether the information on them relates to the research question and provides enough detail about the topic. When students craft paragraphs about their topics, they engage in peer revision and editing and conference with the teacher when necessary. As students draft their Book Creator projects, they receive peer and teacher feedback prior to publication.

Public Products

At the culmination of the research unit, students use the app Book Creator (or a similar app) to publish a digital book, which uses audio, text, images, and video to showcase the information they discover during their research. They share these products with an authentic audience—another class—who evaluates them. As project-based learning experts note, "a public audience is another aspect of authenticity; students are more motivated to produce high-quality work when they know their efforts will have a real-world impact" (Boss & Larmer, 2018, 48). Knowing that their final products would be shared with a different class raises students' level of accountability and motivates them to do their best. Consequently, they create exceptional presentations.

References

Boss, S., & Larmer, J. (2018). *Project based teaching: How to create rigorous and engaging learning experiences*. Alexandria, VA: ASCD.

Fadel, C., Trilling, B., & Bialik, M. (2015). *Four-dimensional education: The competencies learners need to succeed*. Boston, MA: Create Space Independent Publishing Platform.

LESSON 1: Choosing Topics

Estimated Teaching Time: One 45-minute class period

Materials
- writer's notebooks

Driving Question: How do we research and write about a topic of our own choice and share our learning with others?

Critical Question: How do we choose a topic to research?

Warm-Up: In their writer's notebooks, have students generate a list of topics they would like to know more about, want to investigate, or find interesting.

Teaching Steps

1. Direct students to choose three topics from their lists that they like the best.

2. Split the class into two groups: A and B. Have the groups form two lines facing each other (Group A faces Group B).

3. Tell students they will take turns sharing information about each of their potential topics. They will talk about what they already know about the topic, what they want to learn about it, and potential questions they have about it.

4. Have students in Group A talk about their first topic for 45 seconds. If a student runs out of things to say, his or her partner from Group B should ask questions about the topic. After 45 seconds, have students in Group B take a turn to share about their first topic.

5. Next, tell Group A to step to the right to face a new partner. (The student at the end of the line should move to the beginning of the line.)

6. Repeat steps 4 and 5 two more times to discuss students' second and third topics.

7. Ask students to return to their seats and choose the topic that intrigues them the most.

Wrap-Up: In their writer's notebooks, have students record the following about their chosen topic:

- The most important information/idea they shared about it
- Something that puzzles them about it (e.g., a question one of their partners may have asked)
- One or more things they still want to learn about it

A student's list of topics that interest him

LESSON 2: Generating Questions

Estimated Teaching Time: One 45-minute class period

Before You Begin: Prior to starting the lesson, distribute 12-by-18-inch sheets of construction paper and have students make new Pocket Research Organizers for this unit. (See page 12 for instructions.)

Materials
- computers or tablets with internet access
- writer's notebooks
- different-color highlighters
- students' Research Tool Kits (from Chapter 1—Students can use the same ones they created for the "fads" class research project, but they will need to replenish the index cards and replace their used Pocket Research Organizer with a new one.)
- sticky notes
- chart paper

Driving Question: How do we research and write about a topic of our own choice and share our learning with others?

Critical Question: How do we generate research questions to investigate a topic?

Warm-Up: Have students use their computers or tablets to do a quick search of their topic and read an article or two about it. Afterward, tell them to write in their writer's notebooks as many questions about their topic as they can. Direct students to use two different-color highlighters to sort their questions into two categories: those that have short or one-word answers and those that require several sentences or a paragraph to answer. Pair up students and have partners share some questions from each category.

Teaching Steps

1. Ask each student to share a question with the class. If the class thinks it is a one-word-answer question, direct them to hold up one finger. If the class thinks the question demands a paragraph response, tell them to do "jazz hands"—hold up all fingers and rotate the wrist to make the fingers shake.

2. After students finish sharing, ask the class what they notice about the words in the "jazz hands" questions. Guide them to observe that questions requiring paragraph responses often begin with *how* or *why*. Questions that generate one-word answers often start with *who*, *where*, or *when*. *What* questions may also have single-word answers; for example, "What is one type of tide called?" However, some *what* questions may require paragraph responses: "What do the different types of tides do?" Invite students to share some *what* questions and have the class decide whether they require a one-word or a paragraph answer. Ask students who respond to defend their choice.

3. Distribute students' Research Tool Kits. Have students review their questions and revise them as needed. Once they have three questions that require paragraph answers, tell them to write each question on a separate sticky note and place one on each pocket of their Pocket Research Organizer.

4. While you circulate and conference with each student about his or her research questions, have other students jot down answers they already know about their questions on note cards. Remind them to follow the NOTES format:

   N – needs to be own words
   O – organized
   T – topic-related
   E – each card has one fact
   S – short phrases

5. After you have approved students' research questions, have them write their questions directly on the pockets of their organizers (one on each pocket). Then tell them to highlight each question in a distinct highlighter color.

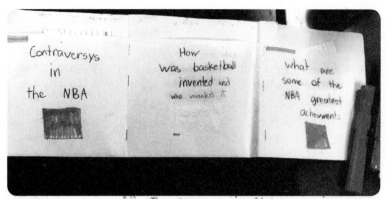

Student's research questions about basketball

Wrap-Up: Distribute a sticky note to each student. On chart paper, write: *How do we generate a good question?* Tell students to write their responses on their sticky note and place it on the chart paper. Remind them to think about the process they used to generate their three research questions and emphasize that their responses should reflect the multiple steps they used.

TIP When conferencing with students about their questions, you may notice that some need to narrow their topic and questions. For example, one of our students chose "cats" as his topic. When we asked him what aspect of cats intrigued him most, he answered, "Their role in Egyptian culture." We suggested that he focus on this particular topic. He then revised his three questions: *What role did Bastet play in Egyptian culture? Why were cats considered to be sacred to Egyptians? What types of cats existed in ancient Egypt?* Conferencing one-on-one with students sometimes works better than teaching a whole-class lesson on how to narrow down a topic because you can listen to what excites them about their topic. As you converse, their three questions begin to unfold.

LESSON 3: Evaluating Sources

Estimated Teaching Time: One 45-minute class period

Before You Begin: Prior to class, check the web links on the PowerPoint presentation "Investigating Websites" to make sure they're still live. (See page 7 for instructions on how to access.) They were still valid at the time of this book's publication, but some may have changed since and need to be replaced.

Materials
- chart paper
- copies of 3Rs Note-Taking Sheet (Reproducible 2A)
- writer's notebooks
- "Investigating Websites" PowerPoint presentation
- copies of Website InspectoRRR Checklist (Reproducible 2B)
- classroom projection system
- notebook paper
- copies of *Two Truths and a Lie: It's Alive!* by Ammi-Joan Paquette and Laurie Ann Thompson, optional (You can purchase discounted copies of this book at **bookdepot.com**.)

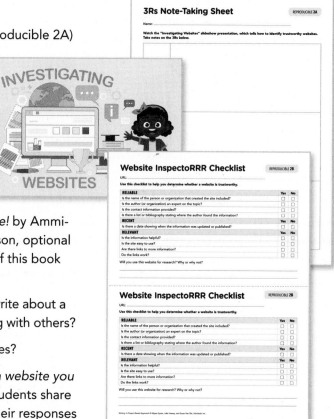

(Available online; see page 7.)

Driving Question: How do we research and write about a topic of our own choice and share our learning with others?

Critical Question: How do we evaluate sources?

Warm-Up: Ask students: *How can you tell if a website you want to use for research is trustworthy?* As students share their thoughts with the class, make a list of their responses on chart paper.

Teaching Steps

1. Distribute copies of the 3Rs Note-Taking Sheet. Tell students to take notes on their sheets as they watch a PowerPoint presentation about how to identify trustworthy websites. (The script for the PowerPoint is in the Notes section of the slides.)

2. Before investigating the website on slide 12 with the class, hand out copies of the Website InspectoRRR Checklist. Ask students to fill out the checklist as you explore the site. Students should check some "noes" on their sheet. As a class, discuss whether or not they should use this site for research. Emphasize that some websites may not meet every criteria on the checklist, but they may still be credible. Slide 17 of the PowerPoint explores a couple of unreliable websites and alerts students to the importance of the 3Rs.

3. As a class, generate three questions that can demonstrate students' understanding of evaluating sources. For example: *What is one thing you learned about evaluating sources? Is it easy or challenging for you to evaluate sources? Why? What questions do you have related to evaluating sources?* Write these on the board.

4. With a student volunteer, model how to ask follow-up questions to attain more information. For example, if the student responds to the first question with, "Be sure a source is credible," ask: *How do you know a source is credible?* This should elicit further responses, such as: "the date is recent; the author has excellent credentials; the suffix domain is .edu"; and so on.

5. Pair up students. Have them take turns asking each other the questions you listed on the board and recording their responses on notebook paper. Tell students they may not repeat the same information their partner presented. Collect these entries to check for understanding.

> **TIP** To save time, number the questions on the board and have students simply number each response instead of writing out each question on the notebook paper. Another viable option is to have students use devices to record the interviews.

1/24

Evaluating sources
1. Some of the domain suffixes are not credible.
Sometimes —   No Way—
.com   .bby
.net
2. Challenging at times when you can't find info like the author, contact us, about us; so she usually looks at all the other credits to see if there's enough.
3. What do you do if it has good info but you can't find the credit? Use best judgment.

These responses reveal the student understands the importance of domain suffixes. She is suspicious of .com and .net sites and will not use blogs. It also shows that finding information about the site, such as the author, can be challenging. Finally, the student realizes that after she checks all the criteria for evaluating websites, she needs to use her own judgment to determine whether it is credible and useful.

Sample student response

Wrap-Up: To provide students with additional practice in evaluating sources, get copies of *Two Truths and a Lie: It's Alive!* by Ammi-Joan Paquette and Laurie Ann Thompson. Divide the class into nine groups and distribute copies of the book. First, direct students to read the Research Guide (near the end of the book) for more tips on how to evaluate websites. Next, assign each group a chapter to read. Tell the class that each chapter contains three articles—two are true, and one is a lie. Explain that each group's job is to read the articles in the assigned chapter and to apply what they have learned about evaluating sources to determine which article is fake. Remind students to look at the bibliography for their assigned chapter and observe the domain suffixes. Ask groups to justify their response in a written paragraph. Afterward, allow students to use the answer key to check their work. If there are discrepancies, discuss why they occurred.

LESSON 4: Conducting Research Independently

Estimated Teaching Time: One 45-minute class period, plus one week in centers

Before You Start: Make multiple copies of the Website InspectoRRR Checklist (Reproducible 2B) and cut them in half. Collate five checklist sheets and staple them into a packet for each student.

Materials

- computers or tablets with internet access
- classroom projection system
- chart paper
- students' Research Tool Kits with Pocket Research Organizers
- packets of Website InspectoRRR Checklist (see Before You Start)
- access to Google Drive and Google Docs
- copies of Cite-Your-Sources Chart (Reproducible 2C), optional
- copies of How to Keep Track of Research (Reproducible 2D)
- writer's notebooks

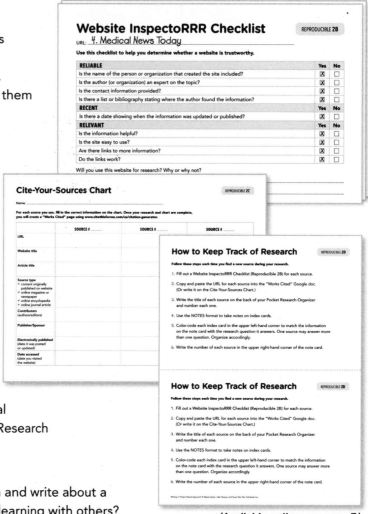

(Available online; see page 7.)

Driving Question: How do we research and write about a topic of our own choice and share our learning with others?

Critical Question: How do we conduct research, keep track of our sources, and take notes?

Warm-Up: Tell students they will begin their independent research today. Remind them that before they can take notes, they must find credible sources. Invite a student to share one of his or her research topics/questions with you. Open a browser, displaying it on the whiteboard, and type into the search bar keywords related to the topic. Have students look at the results and choose a site to review, based on what they learned about picking trustworthy sites from the previous lesson. Click on the suggested site and use it to review the 3Rs. If the site turns out not to be useful or credible, proceed to a second site. Once you find a reliable site, choose a section of the article and model how to take notes. First, remind students what each letter of the NOTES acronym represents (see page 33). Then, skim and scan the article to find a section that answers the student's research question. Ask the class to paraphrase the information and record on chart paper the notes they suggest.

Teaching Steps

1. Direct students to take out their Research Tool Kits and Pocket Research Organizers. Pass out the packets of the Website InspectoRRR Checklist.

2. Tell students to turn on their computers or tablets, go to their Google Drive, open a new Google Doc, and title it "Works Cited." Model how to do this on the whiteboard and have students do it with you as follows:

   - Show students how to click on the + at the top of the browser window to open a new tab. Demonstrate how to type in keywords in the search bar and press enter to conduct the search.
   - Click on a credible website and show students how to select and copy the URL.
   - Then, demonstrate how to click back to the Works Cited tab, type in the number 1, and paste in the URL.

> **TIP** We assume most kids know how to do step 2, but many of our students struggled with simply copying and pasting the URL and toggling back and forth between tabs. Consider using tech-savvy students as teachers or teaching this step in small groups during center time. Alternatively, you can hand out copies of the Cite-Your-Sources Chart for students to record their sources.

3. Display on the whiteboard a copy of How to Keep Track of Research or post an enlarged copy in a prominent place in the room. Tell students to follow the steps as they conduct research and each time they find a new source. (The final three steps are the same as the ones used during the whole-class research project in Chapter 1.)

4. Provide time for students to conduct research, take notes on note cards, and place the note cards in the correct pocket of their organizer.

5. While students are researching, circulate and conference with them. Keep anecdotal records of students' progress and the supports you have provided (e.g., keywords to research, shorter phrases).

Wrap-Up: Project the following prompts on the whiteboard and have students respond to it in their writer's notebooks:

- 3 things I did well during the research process
- 2 things I need to improve when I research
- 1 thing that still confuses me

> **TIP** If you have a limited number of devices available, incorporate research into your language arts centers. For half of the language arts block, one group researches while the rest of the class works on other skills, and then they switch. During this time, differentiate the research instruction and pull out individuals or small groups to work with you. Accommodations can include printing out articles for students who have difficulty reading on the computer, finding articles that align with students' reading levels, and helping students paraphrase.

LESSON 5: Creating a Bibliography

Estimated Teaching Time: One 45-minute class period

Materials

- computers or tablets with internet access
- classroom projection system
- students' Works Cited Google Docs (or Cite-Your-Sources Chart) with a link to a citation generator
- copies of Creating Your Bibliography Online (Reproducible 2E)

Driving Question: How do we research and write about a topic of our own choice and share our learning with others?

Critical Question: How do we cite sources?

Warm-Up: On the whiteboard, display a student's paragraph to read to the class, but put another student's name on it. While giving credit to the wrong student, praise the paragraph's qualities. At this point, the student who wrote the paragraph should object and claim the paragraph as his or her own. Ask students: *How would you feel if someone took your work and claimed it as his or her own?* After listening to their responses, explain that plagiarism is the act of stealing and passing off someone else's ideas or words as one's own. Tell students that to avoid plagiarism, we must always cite our sources to give credit to the true authors.

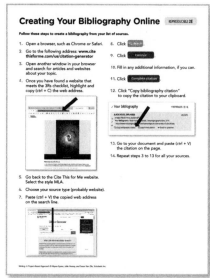

(Available online; see page 7.)

Teaching Steps

1. On the whiteboard, show a credible website related to a research topic. Ask students: *What would you look at to determine if this site is credible?* (Sample answers include author, publisher, date, and title of the article or website.) Tell them this information is similar to the information we need to create our bibliographies.

2. Distribute copies of Creating Your Bibliography Online, which gives step-by-step instructions on how to use the Cite This for Me website (**www.citethisforme.com/us/citation-generator**) to help with citing sources.

3. Model the steps for creating a citation, as listed and demonstrated on the handout. Then, choose a second credible website and have students take turns coming to the whiteboard and showing the class each step to creating a citation.

4. Distribute computers or tablets and direct students to open their Google Drive and go to their Works Cited document, where they pasted the URLs for all their sources.

5. Tell students to copy their first URL, click on the link to the citation generator, and follow the steps on the handout. Remind them how to use the tabs to toggle back and forth between their Works Cited document and the citation generator.

6. When students finish copying and pasting all their citations onto their Google Doc, direct them to arrange the entries in alphabetical order. Use one of the students' documents to model how to do this on the whiteboard.

7. Tell students that the second line of the citation and all subsequent lines should be indented five spaces. Explain that they can also set the hanging indent at ½ inch (model how to do this). Remind them that citations should be double-spaced. Provide time for students to finish formatting their citations.

Wrap-Up: Tell students to turn to a partner and explain how to prevent plagiarism. Then have them share two new pieces of information they have learned about citing sources.

Students use an online citation generator to create their bibliography.

LESSON 6: Revising and Organizing Research Note Cards

Estimated Teaching Time: One 45-minute class period

Materials
- copies of Peer Review for Note-Taking (Reproducible 1C)
- students' Pocket Research Organizers
- paper clips
- sticky notes
- copies of Reflecting on the Research Process (Reproducible 2F)

Driving Question: How do we research and write about a topic of our own choice and share our learning with others?

Critical Question: How do we revise and organize our notes?

Warm-Up: Pair up students. Using the Think-Pair-Share strategy, ask students to think about how they revised and organized their notes for the "fads" class research project (from Chapter 1). After pairs share their thoughts, discuss what students remember about the process.

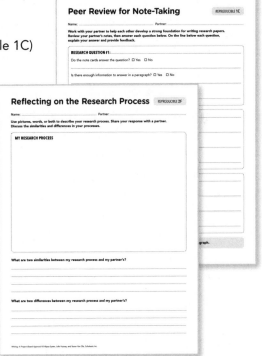

(Available online; see page 7.)

Teaching Steps

1. Distribute copies of the Peer Review for Note-Taking handout and students' Pocket Research Organizers. Review how to evaluate note cards (from Chapter 1, Lesson 4, page 16). Working with a student volunteer, take out the note cards from the first pocket of his or her organizer and spread them out. Model how to determine whether each card relates to the research question on the pocket. If any card does not relate, decide whether it addresses one of the other questions and, if so, put the card in the correct pocket. Discard cards that are off topic.

2. Pair up students. Have students take turns removing the note cards from each pocket of their partner's organizer, spreading them out, and deciding whether the cards belong in that pocket.

3. Next, demonstrate how to determine whether there is enough information in the volunteer's note cards to write a detailed paragraph about the research topic. If more information is needed, suggest keywords the researcher can use to find it. For example, if a student does not have enough information about the different types of tides and what they do, his or her partner might suggest researching the keywords *gravity* and *gravitational pull related to tides.*

4. Finally, continue working with the volunteer to demonstrate how to group cards with related ideas. For example, a student researching the question "How are hiccups created?" may generate three categories of cards related to the question: "diaphragm," "breathing," and "eating and drinking." Tell students to clip together and label the related cards.

5. Circulate as partners conference and complete the handout.

Group note cards with related ideas.

Our Experience: During this process, students make many decisions, and conversations are rich and detailed. One student researching the question "How has interior design changed over time?" had about 60 note cards for this question. With her partner, they organized the information by decades, looked for patterns and key phrases that appeared in each decade, and eliminated changes that appeared in only one source or seemed unimportant. From there, they came up with two or three major changes for each decade and talked through how they would transition from one decade to another without boring the reader. Good-bye, information overload!

In contrast, several students did not have enough information. For example, a student researching the Phillies described Citizens Bank Park as "kid-friendly" but did not elaborate. His partner asked, "What makes it kid-friendly?" and suggested that the researcher address this question.

Other students struggled when grouping their information. A student comparing a mythical unicorn to a Siberian unicorn simply put her cards into two categories: mythical unicorn and Siberian unicorn. Her partner helped her group their differences and similarities. For instance, these creatures have different diets. However, they share some common physical features, such as the horn. Afterward, the researcher had a better understanding of how her information fit together.

Wrap-Up: After students complete their research, distribute copies of Reflecting on the Research Process. Provide time for students to complete it and share their thoughts with a partner. Discuss their observations.

TIP Student reflections provide invaluable information that you can use to drive instruction and to conference. In the first example below, the student needs to learn how to find articles that he can read and understand. Because his notes seemed to be related to his research questions and were easy to group, he comprehended his texts well enough to organize his thoughts. We conferenced with him on selecting appropriate texts. The second student realized she had too many cards that contained limited information. We worked with her on her main idea.

Student Example 1 of "My Research Process"

1. It was kind of difficult because I didn't know what to write down because a lot of info didn't make sense or didn't go with my topic.
2. The card matching with my partner went pretty well, but I needed more information on some of my topics.
3. Matching went pretty well because they [the note cards] all kind of related.
4. Not sure how to start paragraph.

Similarities: We both needed information, and we both got a lot of information.
Differences: He did sports, and I did science. Person and thing.

Student Example 2 of "My Research Process"

This student drew a detailed diagram of her process. The steps delineated are as follows:

1. Researching interior design over time
2. Lay all cards out
3. Group
4. Decide which cards go with [questions] (6–7 cards) (3 groups)
5. Lay the 3 piles out (again) with their groups
6. Decide the transition cards

Good: N-O-T-E-S
Hard: Most of the time too many cards, not much information
Wish: Not so many cards

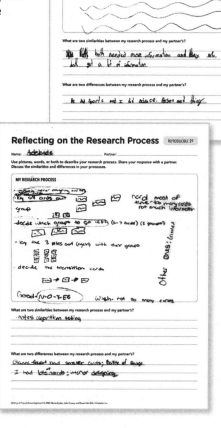

LESSON 7: Using Note Cards to Craft Body Paragraphs

Estimated Teaching Time: One 45-minute class period

Before You Begin: Prior to class, cut 12-by-9-inch black construction paper into four 3-by-9-inch strips. Each student will need two strips.

Materials

- copies of Drafting Checklist (Reproducible 2G), optional
- picture of a sandwich cookie
- black and white construction paper
- writer's notebooks
- copies of Research Paper Rubric (Reproducible 2H)
- computers or tablets with internet access
- students' "fads" class research paper (from Chapter 1)
- access to Google Docs
- Model Research Essay (Reproducible 2I), optional

(Available online; see page 7.)

> **TIP** For students who need additional support with writing, the Drafting Checklist handout provides a means of differentiating instruction.

Driving Question: How do we research and write about a topic of our own choice and share our learning with others?

Critical Question: How do we use notes from different sources to write body paragraphs?

Warm-Up: Form groups of three or four students. Show the class a picture of a sandwich cookie and ask students to discuss this question: *How is this cookie like a paragraph?* Ask groups to share their responses with the class, and record them on the board. Distribute two black strips (see Before You Begin) and one sheet of white construction paper to each student. Have students fold the white construction

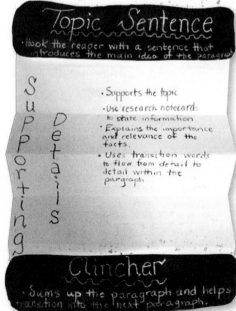

A paragraph "sandwich cookie"

paper horizontally into fourths. Then have them glue one black strip about half an inch from the top of the white sheet and the other black strip about half an inch from the bottom to make a "sandwich cookie." Encourage students to take notes on their sandwich cookie as you explain the different parts. Tell them that the top of the cookie is like the Topic Sentence of a paragraph. Its job is to hook the reader and introduce the main idea of the paragraph. The bottom of the cookie is the Clincher, which sums up the paragraph and helps transition into the next paragraph. In between these two ends are Supporting Details, which support the main idea by providing additional information and explain the importance and relevance of these facts. After students have finished taking notes on their foldable cookie, have them tape it into their writer's notebooks. Tell them to refer to this foldable when they draft their body paragraphs.

Teaching Steps

1. Have students look at their "fads" class research papers (from Chapter 1). Tell them to reread their paragraphs and set a goal for improving the body paragraphs of their own research papers. Ask them to write this goal in their writer's notebooks.

2. Review the steps for using note cards to draft body paragraphs (see Chapter 1, Lesson 5, page 17). If necessary, use your note cards or a student's to model how to draft a body paragraph.

3. Direct students to open a new Google Doc and begin drafting their body paragraphs based on their note cards. As students work, conference with individual students and take anecdotal notes.

TIPS Before students draft, distribute the Research Paper Rubric and review it to acquaint students with the criteria for evaluation. Doing this supports student learning, because at the outset they know the expectations for the final product and can work to fulfill them.

We recommend that throughout the research process, you do everything you ask of your students. Therefore, when reviewing how to draft the body paragraphs, use your own note cards and demonstrate how to draft a paragraph. (See Model Research Essay, in which we use skydiving as our research topic.)

Wrap-Up: Have students reflect on the goals they set in their writer's notebooks and evaluate whether they attained those goals. Remind them to use evidence to support their responses.

LESSON 8: Revising Body Paragraphs

Estimated Teaching Time: One 45-minute class period

Materials

- copies of From Bare Bones to Revision (Reproducible 2J)
- classroom projection system
- ARMS anchor chart (from Chapter 1, Lesson 6)
- printed copies of students' body paragraphs (from Lesson 7)
- red pens
- copies of Revision Checklist for Body Paragraphs (Reproducible 2K)
- students' research papers (Google Docs)

Driving Question: How do we research and write about a topic of our own choice and share our learning with others?

Critical Question: How do we revise our writing?

Warm-Up: Distribute copies of From Bare Bones to Revision. Direct students to read the two paragraphs, paying attention to differences they may observe between the two. For example, the second one adds detail and description, uses vivid verbs, and starts sentences with prepositional phrases. Pair up students and have partners share what they notice.

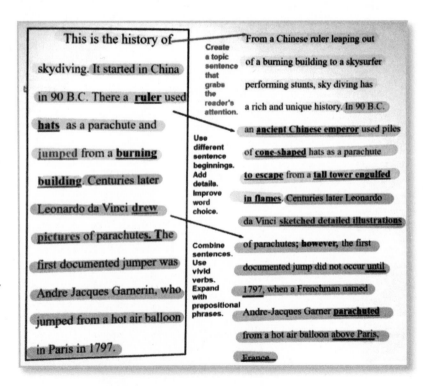

(Available online; see page 7.)

Teaching Steps

1. Display From Bare Bones to Revision on the whiteboard. Invite students to come to the board and talk about their observations. Consider color-coding and highlighting the revision techniques they observe. For example, highlight vivid verbs in yellow, awesome adjectives in pink, and introductory prepositional phrases in green. Add any new revision techniques they noted to the ARMS anchor chart your class created in Chapter 1, Lesson 6.

2. Pass out printed copies of students' drafts and red pens. Direct students to use some of the revision techniques they learned to improve their own paragraphs. Remind them to read each paragraph aloud before making revisions.

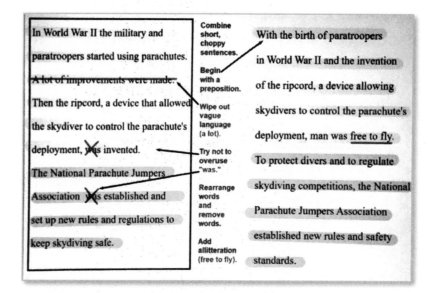

3. After students have finished revising their own work, pair them up with a revision partner. Distribute copies of the Revision Checklist for Body Paragraphs. Review how to use the checklist and provide time for students to evaluate their partner's revisions and then conference with each other.

4. Have students make their revisions on their Google Docs.

Wrap-Up: Ask two or three students to share an example of a sentence before and after revision. Write both sentences on the board and ask the class what revision strategies the writer used. Form groups of three or four students. Instruct students to share "before and after" paragraphs and ask other group members to identify the revision strategy.

> **TIP** After students identify the revision strategies they observe, share the revisions you used to make changes in your own paragraph. Consider using a whole-to-part revision process. Initially, demonstrate a wide variety of revision strategies from which students may choose. As the year progresses, conduct mini lessons based on revision strategies students need or that relate to your grammar instruction. For example, when studying prepositional phrases, you may revisit and target the strategy of starting sentences with prepositional phrases and using them to add detail to sentences.

LESSON 9: Writing the Thesis Statement and Introduction

Estimated Teaching Time: One 45-minute class period

Materials

- large sheets of paper
- computers or tablets with internet access
- students' "fads" class research papers (from Chapter 1)
- copies of Thesis Statement Framework (Reproducible 1F, from Chapter 1, Lesson 8)
- classroom projection system
- individual whiteboards, dry-erase markers, and erasers
- enlarged cutout copies of Model Student Introductions (Reproducible 1D, from Chapter 1, Lesson 8)
- students' research papers (Google Docs)
- copies of Revision Checklist for the Introduction (Reproducible 2L), optional

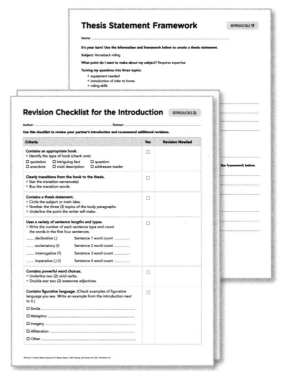

(Available online; see page 7.)

Driving Question: How do we research and write about a topic of our own choice and share our learning with others?

Critical Question: How do we write a thesis statement and introduction?

Warm-Up: Divide the class into groups of three or four students. Hand out a large sheet of paper to each group and instruct them to write down the characteristics of an effective introduction. Discuss their responses as a class.

Teaching Steps

1. Review the definition of a thesis statement (the sentence in the introduction that states the paper's main idea). Then ask students to look at their "fads" class research paper and highlight their thesis statement.

2. Partner students and have them take turns identifying the main idea, three topics, and the writer's intended point in their introductions.

3. Display a copy of Thesis Statement Framework on the whiteboard. Using the topic for your own research paper (or a student volunteer's paper), complete the framework on the board.

4. Distribute copies of the Thesis Statement Framework and provide time for students to complete it using their self-selected topic.

5. Distribute whiteboards, dry-erase markers, and erasers. Ask students to write their thesis statements on their boards and to place them in a circle on the floor when finished. Have students move clockwise around the circle and read each statement silently. Before they reach their own thesis statement, instruct them to evaluate the one in front of them. Have them put a check mark (√) on

the whiteboard if the thesis statement makes sense and contains all the elements, a minus sign (–) if one or more elements is missing, and a question mark (?) if the statement is confusing or does not make sense. When students return to their own statements, pair them up and have partners make suggestions about how to revise each other's thesis statements.

Students evaluate one another's thesis statements.

6. Have students revise their thesis statements based on the feedback they received.

7. Refer students back to the characteristics of an effective introduction that they wrote during Warm-Up. Ask them to think about how they will craft their introductions.

8. To review the types of hooks and transition sentences leading to the thesis statement, post the enlarged Model Student Introductions around the classroom and have students silently reread them. Afterward, ask them to identify the types of hooks used (quotation, intriguing fact, question, anecdote, vivid description, or direct address to the reader), transition sentences, and thesis statements.

> Ballet, an inspirational and difficult art, originated in an interesting way, has a whole dictionary full of steps, and has many appealing reasons for beginning this unique and expressive performing art!

Sample thesis statement

9. Provide time for students to write their own introductions on their Google Doc. Circulate and conference with students as they write.

Wrap-Up: Have students stand up and high-five someone to choose a partner. Direct partners to number themselves 1 and 2. Tell them that while partner 1 reads his or her introduction aloud, partner 2 will do the following:

- draw a hook in the air when he or she hears a hook
- link fingers when a transition is used
- make a T-shape with the hands when the thesis statement is read, lifting one finger on the top hand each time one of the three topics is presented
- share positive comments about the introduction and suggestions for improvement
- switch roles and repeat

TIP For students who need more support or an alternative way of conferencing, partner them up and hand them copies of the Revision Checklist for the Introduction.

Provide time for students to revise their introductions.

LESSON 10: Writing a Conclusion

Estimated Teaching Time: One 45-minute class period

Before You Start: Prior to the lesson, copy and paste eight examples of students' conclusions from the "fads" class research project (Chapter 1, Lesson 10, page 27) onto separate pages of a single document. Enlarge the font. Number each conclusion, print them, and hang them around the classroom.

Materials
- students' conclusions from the "fads" class research project
- paper
- copies of Conclusion Framework (Reproducible 2M)
- classroom projection system
- students' research papers (Google Docs)
- Model Research Essay (Reproducible 2I)
- copies of Revision Checklist for the Conclusion (Reproducible 2N), optional
- computers or tablets with internet access

Driving Question: How do we research and write about a topic of our own choice and share our learning with others?

Critical Question: How do we craft a meaningful conclusion?

Warm-Up: Distribute paper and direct students to number a sheet from 1 to 8. Tell them to walk around the room to read each of the conclusions hanging up. Have them use the following symbols to identify the type of conclusion based on what they learned in Chapter 1, Lesson 10:

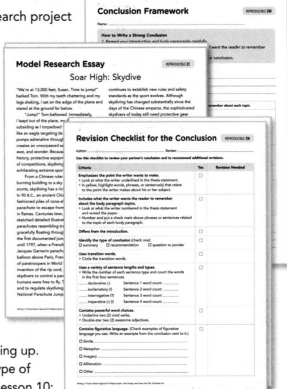

(Available online; see page 7.)

+ = summary

! = recommendation

? = question to ponder

Discuss answers with students and ask them to justify their response.

Teaching Steps

1. Display Conclusion Framework on the whiteboard and distribute copies to students.

2. Tell students that before they can write an effective conclusion, they need to carefully reread their papers. Direct them to open their research papers, reread their introductions, and underline their thesis statements.

3. Explain that in the conclusion, they want to emphasize the point they make in the paper. Therefore, they want to restate the thesis statement in a powerful new way. Use the script in the Teacher Model for Completing the Conclusion Framework (based on our Model Research Essay), next page, to demonstrate how to use the organizer to help them do this. Then, provide time for students to restate their thesis, receive feedback from a partner, and share some of their examples.

4. Using the script in the Teacher Model below, show students how to summarize the ideas of each body paragraph. To scaffold the instruction, pause after each paragraph to provide time for students to fill in their organizers.

Teacher Model for Completing the Conclusion Framework

[Read the introduction aloud.]
As I reread my introduction and think about the point I make in my thesis and paper, I notice that I emphasize the exhilaration and excitement of skydiving. How can I powerfully restate this point? What is it that makes skydiving so exciting? I think it ties into the fact that humans have always had a desire to fly, and skydiving fulfills this dream. I know that's why I tried skydiving. I'm going to use this idea to restate my thesis. I will write: *The thrilling sport of skydiving fulfills humans' desire to soar across the heavens.* This sentence is different from the one in my introduction, and I think it is a strong statement.

The topic of my first body paragraph is the history of skydiving, which I will write on the left side of my organizer. Now, I'm ready to reread each of my body paragraphs and think about what I want the reader to remember. [Read the first body paragraph aloud.] In this paragraph, I want the reader to remember how drastically the sport has changed from the ancient days of the Chinese emperor. On my organizer, I will write this idea: *Sport has changed dramatically.*

The topic of my second paragraph is skydiving equipment, so I will write "equipment" on my organizer. What do I want readers to remember about the equipment? Let me think about this as I reread the paragraph. [Read paragraph 2 aloud.] For me, the most important aspect of the gear is protection. Simple things like gloves, goggles, a helmet, and the parachute, of course, keep the diver safe. On the right side of my organizer, I will write: *Protects diver and makes skydiving safe.*

Body paragraph 3's topic is skydiving competitions. I will write "competitions" on my organizer. As I reread body paragraph 3, I will think about what I want the reader to remember. [Read the paragraph aloud.] What I want to stress here are the variety and range of skydiving competitions. Skydivers can compete in free fall or zero in on a target. On my organizer, I will write: *Wide variety and range.*

Name _____   **Framework for Conclusion**

Restate the thesis (the point you make) in a new way:
The thrilling sport of skydiving fulfills man's desire to soar across the heavens.

What I Want the Reader to Remember About Each Topic

3 Topics of My Body Paragraphs
- history of skydiving
- equipment
- competitions

- Sport has changed dramatically
- protects diver and makes skydiving safe
- wide variety and range

The Last Word/Recommendation/Question to Ponder
The excitement of freefalling at 120 miles per hour, the supreme beauty of the dotted landscape, and the complete freedom of flying make skydiving the adventure of a lifetime.

I want to end my conclusion with a powerful statement that will make the reader say, "Wow!" I want to leave the audience with the sensation of what it is like to skydive, since I have done it and loved it. I'll try describing my favorite part, the free fall, making sure that I do not repeat the description in my introduction. I will say: *The excitement of free-falling at 120 miles per hour, the supreme beauty of the dotted landscape, and the complete freedom of flying make skydiving the adventure of a lifetime.* That's a sentence that drives my point home. I can now use my organizer to write my paragraph.

5. Emphasize that no matter what type of conclusion students choose to write, the last sentence should make a powerful impression on the reader. Use the process described in the Teacher Model for Completing the Conclusion Framework to show students how to think about crafting the final sentence. Provide time for students to write theirs.

6. Have students share their final sentence with three different partners. Then ask the class to nominate some classmates to share their exemplary sentences. Write these sentences on the board and discuss what makes them effective.

7. Additionally, ask students to share a final sentence they want to revise. Write these on the board and have the class suggest revisions.

8. Think aloud to demonstrate how to use the completed organizer to draft the conclusion, as described in the Teacher Model for Drafting the Conclusion below.

9. Provide time for students to use their Conclusion Framework to draft their conclusions on their Google Docs.

Teacher Model for Drafting the Conclusion

To start my conclusion, I could use a transition such as "in conclusion," to let my reader know my paper is ending, but to me, that's like saying, "The end." I like the sentence on my organizer that restates my thesis, so I will write that: *The thrilling sport of skydiving fulfills humans' desire to soar across the heavens.*

To convey my idea about how skydiving has changed throughout history, I need to add in my next sentence some information about how the sport has changed. I know that the Chinese emperor used cone-shaped hats to make a parachute and that paratroopers used the first modern-day parachute. Today, the parachutes sky surfers use are even more sophisticated. How can I put this information into a single sentence? Let me try this: *From a Chinese emperor fashioning cone-shaped hats into a parachute to the paratroopers and sky surfers of the 21st century, the sport of skydiving has changed drastically.* Does that sentence make sense? Yes. If it doesn't, my revision partner can help me fix it. I also think it connects to my

first sentence because it continues to elaborate on the topic of skydiving.

Now, I need to add some specific information about skydiving equipment to the sentence I craft from my organizer. I think I will briefly mention two or three pieces of the safety gear as I summarize. I also need to connect my thoughts about skydiving equipment to my previous sentence. I'll try this: *Throughout history, the basic equipment, such as helmets, goggles, and parachutes, that protects skydivers has also evolved and made skydiving safer.* My transition appears at the beginning of my sentence, and I think it works. I also convey what I want my readers to remember.

This next sentence is more difficult because I must provide some information about the variety of competitions. These competitions can be as open-ended as acrobatic freestyle or as specific as canopy piloting, in which divers land on a target. I also must make sure the sentence naturally flows with what I have already written. How about this: *As a result, divers can feel secure participating in various competitions, such as acrobatic freestyle skydiving or canopy piloting.* I think that works. They must feel safe and secure enough to compete, so I think the transition is effective.

I think the final sentence on my organizer works. Since I am using a summary as my type of conclusion, I just want to provide the last word on my topic here, a statement to wow the reader. Here I will add a transition word that sums up. I will also remove some of the articles (*the*) to make the sentence flow. I'll say: *Overall, the excitement of free-falling at 120 miles per hour, the supreme beauty of the dotted landscape, and the complete freedom of flying make skydiving the adventure of a lifetime.*

Draft of Conclusion

The thrilling sport of skydiving fulfills humans' desire to soar across the heavens. From a Chinese emperor fashioning cone-shaped hats into a parachute to the paratroopers and sky surfers of the 21st century, the sport of skydiving has changed drastically. Throughout history, the basic equipment, such as helmets, goggles, and parachutes, that protects skydivers has also evolved and made skydiving safer. As a result, divers can feel secure participating in various competitions, such as acrobatic freestyle skydiving or canopy piloting. Overall, the excitement of free-falling at 120 miles per hour, the supreme beauty of the dotted landscape, and the complete freedom of flying make skydiving the adventure of a lifetime.

Wrap-Up: Tell students to have their conclusions visible on their screens. Place a number written on a small slip of paper next to each student's computer or tablet. Model how to use the Insert menu on Google Docs to insert a comment. Explain that students will read a conclusion and use the comment feature to compliment the writer or to offer a suggestion for improving the conclusion. Share examples and non-examples of constructive criticism (see below). Instruct students to move to a numbered device, read the conclusion, and comment on it. After students read and review five conclusions, direct them to return to their own and revise their conclusion based on the feedback they've received.

TIP If students have drafted on paper, have them place a large sticky note next to their conclusion for reviewers to write their comments on. You may also have partners use the Revision Checklist for the Conclusion to peer review.

Examples of Constructive Criticism	Non-Examples of Constructive Criticism
The phrase "gory, blood-filled battle" made me shiver. Great use of specific adjectives and alliteration!	I really like your conclusion.
Consider ending with a powerful question rather than a recommendation.	Add more to your conclusion.

LESSON 11: Publishing on Book Creator

Estimated Teaching Time: Two to three 45-minute class periods

Before You Start: Upload Book Creator or a similar app onto your classroom iPads or tablets. Play around with the app to familiarize yourself with it. Consider creating a book yourself to model for students.

Materials
- students' research papers (Google Docs)
- copies of Editing Checklist (Reproducible 2O)
- iPads or tablets with internet connection and Book Creator (or similar) app
- classroom projection system
- chart paper
- model of a completed Book Creator project
- links to students' Book Creator exemplars:
  - Skiing: https://youtu.be/EZLVBQRHaJ4
  - Ballet: https://youtu.be/uwAlpYMsJhY
- copies of Book Creator Planner (Reproducible 2P)
- copies of Book Creator Rubric (Reproducible 2Q)

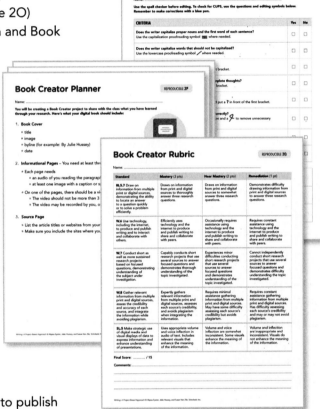

(Available online; see page 7.)

Driving Question: How do we research and write about a topic of our own choice and share our learning with others?

Critical Question: How do we use technology to publish our work and share it with the public?

Warm-Up: Distribute iPads or tablets. If there are not enough devices for everyone, have students work in partners or small groups. Invite students to explore the Book Creator app or a similar one. While they explore, encourage them to discover how to add sound, picture, video, and text. As you circulate, see if anyone has figured out how to do more advanced "moves," such as changing font, color, or backgrounds. After students play with the app, ask them if they have any questions.

> **TIP** Before students publish, provide time for them to edit their papers using CUPS (see Chapter 1, Lesson 7, page 22). They can also use the Editing Checklist to peer-edit one another's papers. Also, throughout the writing process, you can use Google Docs comments to suggest revisions. You can do this independently, or type in your suggestions as you conference with students.

Teaching Steps

1. Call on student "experts" to demonstrate on the whiteboard how to do specific tasks on the Book Creator app.

2. As students teach the class, record the steps for performing each task on chart paper along with the name of the student who is demonstrating. If students forget how to do a task, they can refer to the chart and/or ask the class experts for help.

3. On the whiteboard, show an exemplar of a student's Book Creator project (see YouTube links in Materials). In groups of four, have students discuss the effective and ineffective elements of the presentation. As groups share their responses, create a two-column anchor chart to record their responses.

4. Distribute copies of the Book Creator Planner and Book Creator Rubric to set forth the expectations for the Book Creator project. Provide time for students to create their presentations.

> **TIP** Consider having volunteers come in to escort students to quiet locations for paragraph reading and recording.

Wrap-Up: Tell students to show a person seated nearby one thing they learned or found fascinating about Book Creator.

Reviewing a classmate's Book Creator project

LESSON 12: Presentation and Audience Evaluations

Estimated Teaching Time: Two 45-minute class periods

Materials
- copies of Book Creator Reviews (Reproducible 2R)
- classroom projection system
- model of a completed Book Creator project
- iPads or tablets with internet connection
- writer's notebooks

Driving Question: How do we research and write about a topic of our own choice and share our learning with others?

Critical Question: How do we share our learning with others and evaluate one another's work?

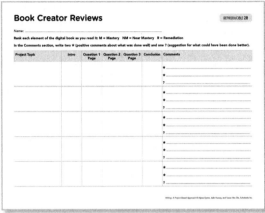

(Available online; see page 7.)

Warm-Up: Pass out copies of Book Creator Reviews. (Each student may need a few copies.) On the whiteboard, show an example of a Book Creator presentation. Have students fill out the evaluation form as they watch the presentation and discuss their responses with a partner. As a class, discuss students' observations.

Teaching Steps

1. Make sure each student has a device on his or her desk with the Book Creator project opened.

2. Instruct students to use the review sheets to critique their peers' presentations.

3. Begin the evaluation process by instructing students to move to a presentation near them.

4. As they finish, they should look for open spaces to watch and evaluate another presentation.

5. After the class finishes their reviews, post students' Book Creator presentations on the school website (or other site) and share them with other classes in the building. Welcome comments and feedback from the wider audience.

Wrap-Up: In their writer's notebooks, have students write down two or three new pieces of information they learned from their peers' presentations and something they want to investigate further. Afterward, have students share with a partner what they wrote.

> **TIP** Depending on the number of devices, you have several options to have students view the Book Creator presentations and evaluate them. You may choose to have the Book Creators uploaded to the internet or Google Drive and create QR codes to hang around the room. This allows partners or a small group of students to view a single presentation with one device. You can also divide the presentations into groups. For example, if you have five devices, five students can display their Book Creator projects at a time. Once all five projects have been evaluated, five new presentations can be displayed. Continue until all presentations have been displayed, viewed, and evaluated.

DESIGNING INFORMATIONAL POSTERS TO COMPARE BOOKS AND MOVIES

Students work on this project partially at home and partially in school. A month before launching this project, have each student pick a book with a movie adaptation to read and watch at home. Given movie ratings, you may need to have parents sign off on their children's book and film choices. As students read their books and watch the movie version, have them fill out the Book-to-Film Graphic Organizers (Reproducible 3A). The graphic organizers will help them begin thinking about how to compare and contrast different elements of the book and the movie. After they finish reading the book and watching the movie, students will continue the project in class, conducting research (e.g., reading and analyzing reviews) and creating web-based informational posters, which will include a rating for the book and the movie and list pros and cons for each one. They will examine how to present different viewpoints to help people make an informed decision about whether to read the book or watch the movie. They will then share their final products with another class. Decision-making is a critical skill for project-based learning, and students experience the process of making a decision as they complete this project.

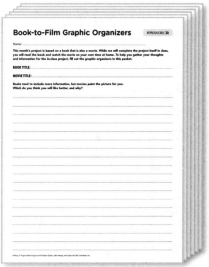

(Available online; see page 7.)

Project-Based Learning Framework

Challenging Problem or Question

Students investigate this driving question: *How do we present balanced viewpoints to help people decide whether to read a book or to watch its movie adaptation?* Throughout this unit, students apply their knowledge of the research process to evaluate reviews to determine the pros and cons of a book and its movie adaptation. After students analyze their findings to help them make their own decision as to which format is better, they have to convey the information they researched to help others do the same.

Sustained Inquiry

To address the driving question, both students and teachers choose a book with a movie adaptation to read and watch together as a starting point. While students initially draw their own conclusions as to which medium they prefer, they consider other factors and opinions before making a recommendation. They conduct research to find book and movie reviews and consult outside perspectives to weigh the pros and cons for both the book and the movie. Questions to research and investigate include the following:

- What strategies can we use to convince others to consider or adopt our personal viewpoints?
- How do we evaluate reviews to determine the pros and cons of a book and its movie version?
- How do we write book and movie summaries?
- How do we critically analyze a book and a movie with a shared story line?
- How do we integrate public reviews and personal opinions to help people make an informed decision?

Authenticity

This project involves authenticity because students engage as critics to produce web-based informational posters that they share with other classes. In our own schools, we shared these projects with the entire school body during our Literacy Night. Attendees used QR codes to access students' informational posters as they walked through the hallways to different literacy activities.

Student Voice and Choice

This project encourages voice and choice from the very start as students independently choose what book and movie they are going to read and watch. As they continue working on the project, they have autonomy in deciding the format of their informational posters and the way in which they display their research. Even though they consult reviewers' viewpoints and opinions, students make their own decisions and recommendations about which is better—the book or the movie.

Reflection

Throughout this unit, we want students to think about the process involved in making an informed decision. In addition, we want students to consider the ideas and input of others, so they also have to reflect upon those viewpoints and what role they play in their final decision. Students respond to the following questions to reflect on the process.

- What process did you engage in to make your decision?
- Did others' viewpoints play a role in your final decision?
- How did you integrate research and personal opinions into making your final decision?

Critique and Revision

Throughout the process, students receive feedback from conferencing with the teacher. In addition, after students fill out their Informational Poster Planners, they complete a peer review to help enhance their content and word choice. After creating their informational posters, students conduct a gallery walk to critique classmates' work and provide feedback before finalizing the project.

Public Products

The autonomy of designing the informational posters and the role of the public audience motivate students. Since their digital posters are going to be published and placed throughout the school for families to view during our schoolwide Literacy Night, our students were driven to impress and put their best work forward.

LESSON 1: Taking a Stance

Estimated Teaching Time: One 45-minute class period

Before You Begin: Prior to starting this unit, choose a book with a movie adaptation for the class read-aloud. (Our class chose *The City of Ember.*) Reading the book and then watching the movie adaptation as a class allows you to model the research process for students.

Materials

- class read-aloud book (see Before You Begin)
- copies of Book-to-Film Venn Diagram (Reproducible 3B)
- chart paper
- copies of Preference Reflection (Reproducible 3C)
- students' completed Book-to-Film Graphic Organizers (see page 55)

Driving Question: How do we present balanced viewpoints to help people decide whether to read a book or to watch its movie adaptation?

Critical Questions

- What strategies can we use to convince others to consider our personal viewpoints?
- How do similarities and differences between a book's and a movie's story lines help people decide which format they prefer?

Warm-Up: Divide the class into two groups—A and B—and have them form two straight lines facing each other. Tell students in Group A they will have 45 seconds to convince the person in front of them to either read a book from their independent book project or watch its movie version. Emphasize that the person will either read the book or watch the movie, but not both. So they need to provide

Book-to-Film Venn Diagram — REPRODUCIBLE 3B

Name:

Compare and contrast the book you read with

Title:

BOOK

Preference Reflection — REPRODUCIBLE 3C

Name:

After filling out the Book-to-Film Venn Diagram, answer these questions.

Title:

1. At the beginning of class, which did you try to convince others is better—the book or the movie? Why?

2. Go back to the Venn diagram in which you listed the similarities and differences between the book and the movie. Highlight the details, scenes, and other elements that you liked best. List them below.

3. In which section did you have the most highlights—the one for the book, the one for the movie, or both?

4. How does this compare to your original argument of which is better? (Did you find that the majority of your highlighting was in the same place as your preference?)

(Available online; see page 7.)

Students try to convince a classmate to either read a book or watch its movie version.

enough information in their 45 seconds to persuade that person to go along with their opinion. When time is up, have students in Group B take a turn. Afterward, have students in Group A move one person to their right (the student at the end of the line will go to the beginning of the line) and repeat the process until each student has had the opportunity to convince three others.

Teaching Steps

1. As students return to their seats, ask if there was anyone who did a really good job of convincing them to either read the book or watch the movie. This helps students focus on the strategies their classmates used.

2. Transition into talking about the class read-aloud book. Have students vote on which they thought was better—the book or the movie version. Then, ask them to defend their stance by providing reasons for their choice.

3. Divide the class into groups of three or four students. Distribute copies of the Book-to-Film Venn Diagram to each group and have students work together to fill it out, comparing the book to the movie.

4. After groups have filled in their organizers, create a class Venn diagram on chart paper and add students' input. Then, discuss the differences between the book and the movie, highlighting those aspects that the class liked better in each format. Guide students to make the connection that it's those differences that help us determine whether we prefer the book or the movie.

Students discuss how a book and its movie version are alike and how they are different.

Wrap-Up: After discussing this connection, distribute copies of the Book-to-Film Venn Diagram and Preference Reflection, as well as students' completed Book-to-Film Graphic Organizers. Using their graphic organizers for reference, have them fill out the Venn diagram to compare and contrast their chosen book to its movie adaptation. As they note the similarities and differences between the two formats, have them complete the Preference Reflection to identify which details, descriptions, or events helped them decide that one is better than the other.

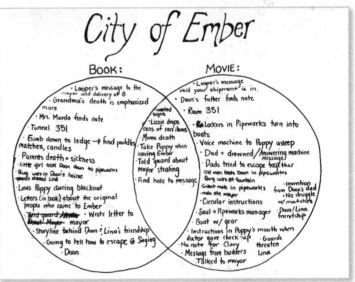

Sample Venn diagram

LESSON 2: Acknowledging Other Viewpoints

Estimated Teaching Time: Two 45-minute class periods

Before You Begin: To model expectations for research, create an enlarged version of the Book and Movie Review Organizer. If you don't have the option to create a poster size of the organizer, you could recreate it on chart paper to use for demonstration purposes.

Materials

- class read-aloud book
- enlarged version of the Book and Movie Review Organizer (Reproducible 3D)
- classroom projection system
- computers or tablets with internet access
- copies of Book and Movie Review Organizer
- writer's notebooks

Driving Question: How do we present balanced viewpoints to help people decide whether to read a book or to watch its movie adaptation?

Critical Question: How do we evaluate reviews to determine the pros and cons of a book and its movie version?

Warm-Up: Remind students that in the previous lesson, we expressed our preferences about whether the class read-aloud book or its movie adaptation is better. In groups of four, have students discuss their own opinions and see if everyone in their group agrees. As students discover that different thoughts and opinions will always exist, circulate from group to group and ask why this is the case. Transition from the group discussions to a whole-class conversation, and then ask how we can incorporate other people's thoughts and opinions to help us make an informed decision.

Teaching Steps

1. As a class, discuss how to include and reference other people's input when writing a review. Ask students: *Where can we find reviews for books and movies?*

2. Use the class read-aloud book to model how to research and find common themes in reviews. Use a preferred review website to read and collect information (see Tip, page 60). Begin by finding the overall average rating for the book and recording

(Available online; see page 7.)

it on the enlarged Book and Movie Review Organizer. As you read the reviews to the class, think aloud while taking notes that reference similar pros and cons on the chart. (See Teacher Model.)

Teacher Model

As we search through Goodreads, we want to look for comments and reviews that make similar remarks. For now, I am going to scroll through and read the posts; however, I noticed that I also have the option of sorting the reviews based on the ratings and stars reviewers have given. Before we look at that, I want to make a note of the average rating that reviewers have given the book. It looks like the average rating is 3.86 (out of 5 stars), so I am going to record that in my organizer.

I notice that a lot of people mentioned that the book had a creative and well-developed setting, so I am going to list these comments in the pros section of my graphic organizer. I have also read a few comments about how the story line was very predictable and didn't require any imagination. I agree with this as well, since throughout the whole story there really aren't any twists or turns that lead to problems finding the way out of Ember. So I'm going to list this in the cons section of our organizer. The rest of the comments seem to mention how they liked the cliff-hanger ending, vivid descriptions throughout the book, and how Ember gave insight into living in a simplistic manner. We should include these in the pros as well.

It seems as if most readers really enjoyed *The City of Ember*, but we must remember that everyone has different insights, opinions, and likes, so we have to include things that people did not like about the book as well. Since we are not seeing a lot of reviews that mention dislikes, I am going to go back and sort the reviews so we see comments and reviews from people who rated the book as one star. This will help us narrow our search.

Now I see that a lot of people felt the characters were very flat. This means that throughout the book, the characters are very one-dimensional and don't really change. I can see how people could feel this way, as the personalities, emotions, and characteristics of both Doon and Lina remain consistent throughout the book. I am also reading a lot about how they felt the author was redundant in her storytelling. It appears reviewers felt that she repeated herself and would explain too much, leaving little room for inferencing. We will have to list these in the cons on our organizer as well.

We seem to have covered most of the reviews and comments listed on Goodreads and have integrated both positive and negative aspects of the book. However, we must remember that we need to include input from multiple sources, just as we did when we gathered information for our independent research. I feel confident in the information we have gathered so far. Now it's time to look somewhere else.

3. Continue involving the class in the process. Invite students to raise their hands when they notice a common theme or similarities in various reviews and put those thoughts in their own words to add to the class Review Organizer.

4. After filling in the Goodreads review for the class book, divide the class into groups of two or three students. Assign each group a part of the class organizer, so that members are responsible for filling out a review site for either the book or the movie, including the average rating, pros, and cons.

TIP Goodreads, Common Sense Media, and Amazon are good options for book reviews. These resources plus Plugged In are helpful for movie reviews as well. If none of these sites has the books or movies students choose to use, have them use a search engine to find additional review websites.

5. After all of the groups have completed their portion of the review research, bring the class together and record their observations on the class organizer.

6. Distribute copies of the Book and Movie Review Organizer to students. Provide time for them to complete their individual organizers for their chosen book and movie.

Wrap-Up: In their writer's notebooks, have students respond to the following.

- What reviews did you read that struck you most and why?
- Were there any reviews that you completely agreed or disagreed with? Why?
- Is it important to include reviews you don't agree with? Why?

Students read and evaluate reviews online.

LESSON 3: Drafting Informational Posters

Estimated Teaching Time: One 45-minute class period

Materials

- students' completed Book-to-Film Venn Diagrams (from Lesson 1)
- students' completed Book-to-Film Graphic Organizers (see page 55)
- copies of Informational Poster Planner (Reproducible 3E)
- chart paper or whiteboard
- students' completed Book and Movie Review Organizers (from Lesson 2)
- writer's notebooks
- copies of Informational Poster Rubric (Reproducible 3F)

Driving Question: How do we present balanced viewpoints to help people decide whether to read a book or to watch its movie adaptation?

(Available online; see page 7.)

Critical Questions:

- How do we write story-line summaries for a book and a movie?
- How do we critically analyze a book and a movie with a shared story line?

Warm-Up: Have students review the Book-to-Film Venn Diagram they completed in Lesson 1. Ask them to think about and decide whether there are enough similarities to write a summary that describes both their self-chosen book and its related movie. If there are not enough similarities, have them refer back to their Book-to-Film Graphic Organizers to help them list additional information that includes the major elements of the plotlines for both book and movie.

Teaching Steps

1. Distribute copies of the Informational Poster Planner. Tell students their job is to help others make an informed decision about whether to read their chosen book or watch the movie. They'll do this by providing the story line, their thoughts and opinions, and reviewers' comments.

2. Using the class read-aloud book, model how to write a summary that includes the story line of both the book and the movie by focusing on the similarities in the Venn diagram. At the same time, emphasize the importance of making the summary entertaining to pull in readers or viewers.

> ### Sample Story-Line Summary
> In *The City of Ember*, Lina Mayfleet and Doon Harrow live in a close-knit, shadowy city where the only beams of light come from the lanterns hanging above. As they question the integrity of their city, the number of blackouts Ember experiences skyrockets, causing Lina and Doon to want to find a way out. Their hope quickly increases as they find the Instruction for Egress (Exit), but then plummets as Lina's little sister chews on the paper, leaving them with only bits and pieces of what they need. To keep their dreams alive, they work together to try to escape through the Pipeworks below the city. Despite many twists and turns along the way, it still seems as though there is light at the end of the tunnel.

3. Direct students to use their completed Venn diagrams to help them write their individual summaries with a focus on the similarities between their book and the related movie, including common plotlines. While students write on the first page of their Informational Poster Planner, walk around and conference with individuals about their work.

4. After students have completed their summaries, model how to use the pros and cons from their Book and Movie Review Organizers to analyze and summarize other reviewers' thoughts and opinions.

5. Direct students to use this process to write their own analyses of reviews on the second and third pages of their Informational Poster Planner.

Wrap-Up: Distribute copies of the Informational Poster Rubric and have students use it to rate their drafts. In their writer's notebooks, have students reflect on how using others' input and public reviews to provide a recommendation is better than using just one person's thoughts and opinions.

LESSON 4: Revising Informational Posters

Estimated Teaching Time: One 45-minute class period

Materials

- students' completed Informational Poster Planners (from Lesson 3)
- sticky notes
- students' completed Informational Poster Rubric (from Lesson 3)
- copies of Review Analyses Revision Checklist (Reproducible 3G)
- writer's notebooks

Driving Question: How do we present balanced viewpoints to help people decide whether to read a book or to watch its movie adaptation?

Critical Question: How do we revise our writing?

Warm-Up: Review with students the important aspects that should be included in their Informational Poster Planner. Ask them to turn to a partner and discuss ways they could improve their summaries and review analyses. As students discuss, have them write on a sticky note one area they really want to focus on when revising, based on how they rated themselves with the rubric in the previous lesson.

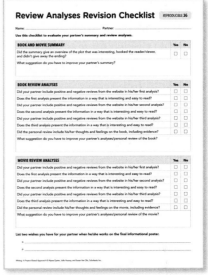

(Available online; see page 7.)

> **TIP** Prior to choosing which student work to revise, read through some student examples and choose one that has errors common to the class. This will help provide support and input for others as well.

Teaching Steps

1. To make revisions authentic, ask for a student volunteer who would like the class's help in revising his or her review analysis.

2. Using teacher think-aloud and student support, provide input and suggest revisions for one of the student's review analyses.

3. Pair up students and distribute to each student a copy of the Review Analyses Revision Checklist. Have partners review each other's Informational Poster Planner and use the checklist to offer suggestions for improving their partner's summaries and reviews.

Students help each other improve their summaries and reviews.

4. Afterward, have students revise their summary and analyses based on their partner's feedback.

Wrap-Up: In their writer's notebooks, have students write one revision that they feel made a difference to their overall product and why that was the case.

LESSON 5: Designing a Web-Based Informational Poster

Estimated Teaching Time: One to two 45-minute class periods

Before You Start: Review various websites for creating informational posters, such as Venngage, Piktochart, Easel.ly, and Canva. (For each of these websites, there is an option to create an account through Google.) After you have chosen which site you want your class to use, allow students to play around with the website during center time to familiarize themselves with how to add text, pictures, backgrounds, and information. This will help save time during the class period so students can focus on creating their informational poster instead of learning how to use the website.

Materials

- students' completed Informational Poster Planner (from Lesson 4)
- computers or laptops with internet access
- classroom projection system
- links to student examples:
  - https://bit.ly/363OVo7
  - https://bit.ly/2YqoSov
  - https://bit.ly/2LpXP7x
  - https://bit.ly/38735GK
- copies of Informational Poster Response Sheet (Reproducible 3H)
- sticky notes
- copies of Informational Poster Rubric (Reproducible 3F)

(Available online; see page 7.)

Driving Question: How do we present balanced viewpoints to help people decide whether to read a book or to watch its movie adaptation?

Critical Questions

- How do we critically analyze a book and a movie with a shared story line?
- How do we integrate public reviews and personal opinions to help other people make an informed decision?

Students familiarize themselves with a website for creating informational posters.

Warm-Up: Have students get together in groups of four to discuss what information would help people decide whether to read a book or to watch its movie adaptation. Continue this conversation as a class by asking students to point out the parts in their Informational Poster Planners that would help people make an informed decision. Once they have noted that they would need multiple viewpoints and information from sources—positives and negatives from both, average ratings, and a recommendation—display examples of other students' informational posters on the board (see links in Materials).

Teaching Steps

1. Allow students time to create their informational posters online for their book and its related movie.

2. As students work on their posters, conference with them individually to provide input and feedback.

3. Once all students have completed their online posters, have them participate in a gallery walk. Place a copy of the Informational Poster Response Sheet next to each poster for viewers to fill out. As students view classmates' work, have them fill out the reflection to acknowledge things they liked and to make recommendations for improving the overall product.

4. As soon as each student has between 5 and 10 viewers who have provided feedback, allow the class time to make any changes they feel are necessary to improve their overall product.

> **TIP** We have found that it can be difficult for students to create and format their web-based informational posters when using an iPad. For this part of the project, you may want to provide students with laptops so they can create and design with less struggle.

Viewing and critiquing a classmate's online informational poster

Wrap-Up: Pair up students to look at each other's informational poster. In doing so, they should write on a sticky note one suggestion and one compliment. If time allows, continue this process so that students have input from at least two or three peers. Have students make any necessary changes on their posters, based on feedback. After students have finalized their posters, use the Informational Poster Rubric to assess their work.

> **TIP** After completing this unit, consider downloading each student's informational poster and creating a QR code for others to access it. You can invite other classes to view the final product, so they can get recommendations for other books to read or movies to watch. Our school also hosts a Literacy Night and invites all families to attend. We hang up the QR codes for people to access and view as they transition among activities.

CREATING CAMPAIGNS TO PROMOTE NUTRITIOUS FOODS

In this unit, students continue to hone their research and technology skills as they investigate nutritious fruits and vegetables. They use facts from their research to write a campaign speech in a five-paragraph persuasive essay format from the food's point of view. Students draw a picture of their food and use the web 2.0 tool Blabberize to animate the image and make it talk. (Blabberize allows students to record their voices and practice their speaking skills without standing in front of a live audience.) They then share their final products with other classrooms. To motivate students to do their best work, consider inviting other classes to vote on the most nutritious food, based on the presentations.

While this unit requires students to write a five-paragraph persuasive essay, you can modify the project so they only write the introduction and conclusion for the Blabberize presentation and speak from their note cards. Alternatively, they can simply write a paragraph justifying why their food is the most nutritious.

Project-Based Learning Framework

Challenging Problem or Question

Students investigate this driving question: *How do we persuade the public that a particular fruit or vegetable's health benefits make it the most nutritious food?* This question sets the purpose for learning and allows students to utilize their knowledge of research to gather information and integrate facts to persuade an audience.

Sustained Inquiry

To address the driving question, both students and teachers activate their prior knowledge to identify what makes a food "healthy" and to convince others to adopt their opinion about which fruit or vegetable is the most nutritious. Throughout the process, students conduct research to investigate the nutritional value of their chosen food, determine its health benefits, and use their research to persuade others that their fruit or vegetable is the healthiest option. During this project, students incorporate persuasive techniques, taking on the persona of their fruit or vegetable. In the end, they present their information from the food's perspective and prepare a campaign speech to practice public-speaking skills. Questions requiring research and investigation include the following:

- What makes a food healthy?
- How do we use nutritional facts about fruits and vegetables to determine their health benefits?
- How do we sort and organize related information?
- How do we assume the perspective of a fruit or vegetable?
- How do we integrate persuasive techniques with factual information to influence an audience's vote?
- What is a persuasive speech, and how do we write one?

Authenticity

The task of integrating researched information to persuade an audience makes this project authentic. The use of technology to deliver the content is a 21st-century skill. Since other students or classes vote for the most nutritious food, the audience extends beyond the classroom into the larger community.

Student Voice and Choice

In this project, students exercise their own voice and choice by selecting a fruit or vegetable, designing a character to represent their food choice, and creating a persona to represent the voice of their character. Although planners, organizers, rubrics, and conferences guide students' work, each student ultimately has autonomy over how he or she delivers the information to promote the nutritional facts and health benefits of his or her chosen food.

Reflection

When faced with the task of persuading others, students need to continually reflect on how the audience will perceive the information based on their understanding of who the audience is. Throughout this project, students reflect on the process by responding to the following prompts.

- Describe the process you used to investigate your food.
- Give details about how you organized your information.
- Explain how you incorporated persuasive techniques to create your campaign speech.

Critique and Revision

During this project, students receive feedback from conferencing with the teacher, peer evaluation of note-taking sheets, and peer revision of their campaign speeches. Students and teachers also use Google Docs' comments to improve the project's content and formatting. Additionally, students consult with their peers when choosing their food's voice and employing speaking skills. Based on this feedback, they adjust their word choices, ideas, and voice in their speeches prior to recording them.

Public Products

Throughout the unit, students are not only motivated by the autonomous nature of their speeches, but they are also driven by the natural competition and the role of an outside audience. Since they have the opportunity to share their final product with other classes, students take great interest in showcasing their hard work.

LESSON 1: Brainstorming and Taking Notes

Estimated Teaching Time: One 45-minute class period, plus a week for researching facts during center rotations

Before You Start: Prior to starting the unit, choose your own fruit or vegetable to model the research and writing process for your class. While we have included our own research notes and essay about okra for modeling purposes, you may want to use your own notes and essay. We find that going through the process with students makes the learning authentic and allows them to see that writing isn't always easy—even for teachers!

Materials

- *Sesame Street* clips about healthy foods:
  - https://youtu.be/KBMxpDbp51A
  - https://youtu.be/pEvhJKwxsZk
- classroom projection system
- copies of an article about a fruit or vegetable of your choice (For our okra model, we used this online article: https://bit.ly/33X5iBb)
- copies of Research and Resource Graphic Organizer (Reproducible 4A)
- copies of Fruit and Vegetable Choices (Reproducible 4B)
- computers or tablets with internet access

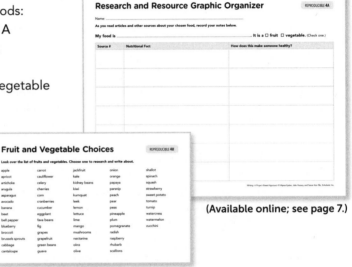

(Available online; see page 7.)

Driving Question: How do we persuade the public that a particular fruit or vegetable's health benefits make it the most nutritious food?

Critical Questions:

- What makes a food healthy?
- How does the public use nutritional facts about fruits and vegetables to determine their health benefits?

> **TIP** When printing the Research and Resource Graphic Organizer, make sure to print it one-sided, as students will be cutting the facts into individual slips in a later lesson.

Warm-Up: Using the links provided above, watch with the class the *Sesame Street* clips about healthy foods. Afterward, talk about what makes a food healthy.

Teaching Steps

1. Ask students to name examples of foods that are healthy. Record their responses on the board. Tell students that they will choose a fruit or vegetable to research and eventually write a persuasive speech or essay to convince others that their food is the most nutritious.

2. Distribute copies of an article about your fruit or vegetable and use it to guide students through the note-taking process. Remind them of the note-taking skills they learned during the research unit (i.e., NOTES acronym in Chapter 1, Lesson 2, page 13).

3. To model note-taking, display on the board a copy of the Research and Resource Graphic Organizer. Then read the article aloud to the class. As you read, make notes on the graphic organizer about nutritional facts and the health benefits related to these facts. (See Teacher Model below.) Tell students it's important to stress the health benefits, because this part of the research will help with writing the persuasive speech.

Teacher Model

You have a copy of my source #1 article. Any notes I take from this article will be marked as "1." Let's read the first few sentences: *Okra provides ample calcium and magnesium, helping prevent both calcium and magnesium deficiency. In addition to healthy bones, calcium is needed to regulate heart rhythms, blood pressure, and cholesterol levels.*

Wow! That's a lot of BIG words. Let's see... first, I need to write "1" under "Source #."

Next, I need to write the nutritional fact: *Okra has plenty of calcium.* I think I need to reread what calcium does. If the article doesn't tell me, I will need to do additional research as to why calcium is important. Will someone read the sentences again for me? Oh, so calcium helps control heart rhythms, blood pressure, and cholesterol. It also builds up bones. I will write that under the "How does this make someone healthy?" column.

4. As you model the note-taking process, invite students to give input about nutritional facts and health benefits.

5. Afterward, hand out copies of Fruit and Vegetable Choices and the Research and Resource Graphic Organizer. Have students choose a food from the list of choices, then discuss your expectations on how and when research will be done. Again, emphasize the importance of gathering not just nutritional facts about their food choice, but also including the health benefits associated with those nutritional facts.

Students take notes on their organizers as they read articles about their chosen foods.

6. Allow students time to begin researching their fruit or vegetable independently and taking notes on their graphic organizer.

Wrap-Up: Pair up students and have them share one fact about what makes their chosen food healthy and how it benefits the body.

Students share facts about their chosen foods.

> **TIP** We have found that students often have difficulty finding health benefits that correlate with the nutritional facts. As students do research independently, take time to conference with individuals to make sure they are writing about why their chosen food is healthy and how it benefits the body and a healthy lifestyle. For example, "contains calcium," doesn't explain how calcium benefits the body or makes one healthy, but the following does: "Contains calcium, which your body needs to build and maintain strong bones. Your heart, muscles, and nerves also need calcium to function properly. Some studies suggest that calcium, along with vitamin D, may have benefits beyond bone health, perhaps protecting against cancer, diabetes, and high-blood pressure."

LESSON 2: Organizing Notes

Estimated Teaching Time: One 45-minute class period

Before You Start: Prior to beginning this lesson, create 4-Pocket Research Organizers for students (or have them make their own). Follow the steps from Chapter 1, Lesson 1 (page 12), but create four pockets (instead of three) by stapling the folded sheet of construction paper about 4½ inches apart. The additional pocket will be for "Other" facts.

Also, cut apart your research notes (or the Okra Example Notes, Reproducible 4C) into strips and sort the facts into three or four categories, placing them in your own 4-Pocket Research Organizer.

Materials

- copies of teacher's research notes for chosen food (or Okra Example Notes, Reproducible 4C), for each group of students
- scissors for each student
- students' completed Research and Resource Graphic Organizers (from Lesson 1)
- 4-Pocket Research Organizer for each student (see Before You Start)

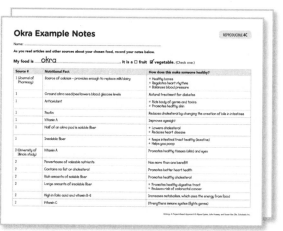

(Available online; see page 7.)

Driving Question: How do we persuade the public that a particular fruit or vegetable's health benefits make it the most nutritious food?

Critical Question: How do we sort and organize related information?

Warm-Up: Divide the class into small groups. Give each group one set of your research notes (or the Okra Example Notes) and scissors. Instruct students to cut apart the facts from the research notes and sort the strips into three or four categories, each with a common theme. After students have sorted the facts, discuss the categories they generated. For example, categories for okra could be: prevents diseases, helps heal sicknesses, aids digestion, and other. Invite students to share their reasons behind their groupings. Then model and explain how you grouped your facts and why.

Teaching Steps

1. Distribute students' filled-out Research and Resource Graphic Organizers. Have them cut their facts into strips.

2. Tell students they should aim to group their facts into three categories. Explain that each category will be a reason that supports their argument as to why their food is the most nutritious. Emphasize that it's okay to have facts left over in a fourth pile. This fourth pile will be placed in the "Other" pocket of their organizers. The facts in the "Other" pile could be useful when they write the introduction and conclusion.

Students cut apart their notes into strips.

3. Distribute the 4-Pocket Research Organizers to students. Have students put related notes into a pocket and label the pocket with its category (or reason).

4. Next, pair up students to share their categories with each other. During this time, encourage students to critique and help each other revise their categories to solidify them and make sure the related facts fit within those categories.

Wrap-Up: Have students find a new partner to share their three categories/reasons. While students share, they should look for similarities among categories and discuss whether or not their fruits or vegetables share nutritional facts that suggest common themes.

TIP While students share with partners, circulate and conference with individuals to help them find a main idea among the related information. Conferencing also provides guidance for struggling students, and helping them organize information now will prove beneficial when it is time to write the body paragraphs.

Students sort their strips into categories.

LESSON 3: Taking on a Perspective

Estimated Teaching Time: One 45-minute class period

Materials
- plain white paper
- markers and crayons
- writer's notebooks
- classroom projection system
- speech examples:
  - Onion: https://bit.ly/2qoGdl4
  - Mango: https://bit.ly/2s2ziyE

Driving Question: How do we persuade the public that a particular fruit or vegetable's health benefits make it the most nutritious food?

Critical Question: How do we assume the perspective of a fruit or vegetable?

Warm-Up: Using the links provided above, watch the sample onion and mango speeches with the class. Ask students what they notice about the speeches. Specifically, have them focus on the voice and appearance of each food to guide them toward the idea of taking on a perspective other than their own.

Teaching Steps
1. Explain to students that in this unit, they will create their own persona for the food they have chosen and researched. Just as in the videos they watched, they will give their food a voice to explain its nutritional value. At the end of the unit, they will take part in an election process, in which students will decide which fruit or vegetable is the most nutritious food choice.

2. Hand out paper, markers, and crayons to students. Have them draw a colorful and personified image of the food they researched. Remind them that since the food will be talking, it will need a mouth!

3. Direct students to look at the pictures they have created. Remind them that they will make their foods come to life and try to convince others to vote for them. In their writer's notebooks, have them list the personality traits they want their food to portray through their campaign speeches. (Students will work on their foods' voices in a later lesson.)

Students' drawings of personified fruits and vegetables

TIP After students create their colorful and personified image of their food, photograph each one. Place each photo in a file folder on Google Drive so students can access theirs when it's time to create the speech on Blabberize.

4. For this lesson's final step, have students come up with names for their foods. This is a great time to review how to use alliteration when creating names as a persuasive technique. Remind students that they want the voters to remember their food's name when it's time to vote.

Wrap-Up: Have students form a circle with their pictures. One at time, have them show their picture to the class and announce their food's name.

Invite students to introduce their fruit or vegetable characters to the class.

LESSON 4: Developing Body Paragraphs

Estimated Teaching Time: One to three 45-minute class periods

Materials
- teacher's 4-Pocket Research Organizer with organized notes
- classroom projection system
- teacher's essay (or Okra Sample Essay, Reproducible 4D)
- students' 4-Pocket Research Organizers with organized notes
- computers or tablets with internet access
- writer's notebooks or Google Docs

Driving Question: How do we persuade the public that a particular fruit or vegetable's health benefits make it the most nutritious food?

Critical Question: How do we integrate persuasive techniques with factual information to influence an audience's vote?

Warm-Up: Divide the class into groups of four and ask students to brainstorm what makes a spectacular paragraph. Listen to their ideas and list the components on the board or on chart paper. The list should include: a topic sentence, supporting details with explanations, a clincher sentence, and transitions.

Okra Sample Essay

REPRODUCIBLE 4D

Hello, I am Oakley the Outstanding Okra. According to the University of Illinois, I am a "powerhouse of valuable nutrients." That means I'm a highly nutritious food. You might not recognize me in my natural emerald, spiky-finger shape. Most people see me when I am sliced into my signature star shape and then fried, boiled, or pickled. One (non-fried) serving of me is healthy and tasty, for I am a fat- and cholesterol-free food that contains only 30 calories. I, Oakley the Outstanding Okra, am the most nutritious food because when you eat me, I help prevent diseases, act as medication, and rid the body of wastes.

Numerous people get sick every day with a common cold or even a disease. What if the food you ate gave your body the nutrition it needs to prevent these sniffling, runny-nose instigators or debilitating diseases from attacking? Well, look no further. I, Oakley the Okra, am full of nutrients and vitamins that have this germ-fighting superpower! One cup of me contains 22 percent of the recommended daily allowance of natural folates. Folates (when in their natural state) decrease cancer risks, according to a study conducted by Medical News Today. Okra—that's me—also boosts immune systems and prevents colds, because I contain 36 percent of the recommended daily allowance of vitamin C. Vitamin C fights off radicals (also known as germs) by creating more white blood cells. As you can see, okra, like me, needs to be added to your diet for your body to reap the benefits of vitamin C and folates.

Not only do I prevent disease, but one serving of me can also treat your medical problems. In ancient times, before medicine was even around, people used my okra leaves as pain relief and as a treatment for depression. Today, lots of people suffer from depression. If you are one of them, I can help you. The Mazandaran University of Medical Science experimented and found okra seed extracts, which are high in phenol and flavonoid content, work like the current antidepressant medications on the market. So to stop feeling blue, eat me! Ground okra seed and peel also lowers blood glucose levels based on a study reported by the Journal of Pharmacy. My okra pods also contain myricetin, which alleviates the effect of diabetes by increasing sugar absorption in muscles to lower blood sugar. In 2005, Jilin Medical Journal wrote that my okra friends and I reduce uric acid and protein in urine, which helps people with kidney disease.

Writing: A Project-Based Approach © Myrna Epstein, Julia Massey, and Susan Van Zile, Scholastic Inc.

(Available online; see page 7.)

Teaching Steps
1. Take out your 4-Pocket Research Organizer and pull out the facts for your category/reason 1. Display your facts on the board and think aloud the process of composing a paragraph. Model how to determine a topic sentence for all the facts. Continue modeling the supporting details and clincher sentence. (See Teacher Model, next page.)

Teacher Model for Body Paragraph 1

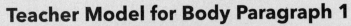

I think I'll start with the "prevents diseases" pocket. I have many facts about okra preventing sickness and boosting the immune system. First, I need to grab attention. How many of you like being sick? Me neither. So, what if I start my paragraph with: *Do you like getting sick? If you eat me, you won't get sick!* Remember, we're writing from the food's perspective, so that's why I'm using the pronoun *me*. What do you think about this claim, though? Is it true? Hmm, probably not 100 percent true. Is this more accurate? *Eating okra will help you fight off many germs.*

Now, I need a fact that supports or proves this to be true. I have a fact that says okra has vitamin C, which fights radicals, also known as germs. So, how about this? *Do you like getting sick? If you eat me, you will be fighting off many germs. Okra—that's me—boosts your immune system and prevents colds with 36 percent of the recommended daily allowance of vitamin C. Vitamin C also fights off radicals (also known as germs) by creating more white blood cells.*

Looking at my facts, I see that a study has shown that okra's folates decrease cancer risks. Let me add that: *Folates (when in their natural state) decrease cancer risks, according to a study conducted by Medical News Today.*

Now I need a clincher sentence: *As you can see, you need to add me to your diet for your body to get the benefits of vitamin C and folates.*

Let's see how my paragraph sounds after I have revised it.

Model Body Paragraph 1

Do you like getting sick? If you eat me, you will be fighting off many germs. Okra—that's me—boosts your immune system and prevents colds with 36 percent of the recommended daily allowance of vitamin C. Vitamin C also fights off radicals (also known as germs) by creating more white blood cells. Folates (when in their natural state) decrease cancer risks, according to a study conducted by Medical News Today. As you can see, you need to add me to your diet for your body to get the benefits of vitamin C and folates.

2. Share the rest of your essay with the class.

3. Afterward, distribute students' 4-Pocket Research Organizers and have students write a paragraph for their category/reason #1 in their writer's notebooks or on Google Docs. (If they use Google Docs, remind them to share it with you for electronic feedback.)

TIP Given our schedule, we found it beneficial to compose one paragraph a day. Depending on your schedule, drafting all three paragraphs in one class period may be feasible.

4. While students draft their first body paragraphs, circulate and conference with individuals.

5. Continue this process for body paragraphs 2 and 3.

Wrap-Up: Pair up students and have partners share their paragraphs with each other. Each partner should be able to identify the topic sentence, reasons and evidence with explanations, and the clincher sentence. If a paragraph is missing an essential ingredient, students will need to revise.

Using organized notes to compose a paragraph

LESSON 5: Writing Introductions

Estimated Teaching Time: One 45-minute class period

Materials
- speech examples
    - Onion: https://bit.ly/2qoGdl4
    - Mango: https://bit.ly/2s2ziyE
- classroom projection system
- copies of Thesis Statement Planner (Reproducible 4E)
- teacher's 4-Pocket Research Organizer with organized notes
- students' 4-Pocket Research Organizers
- copies of Speech Introduction Planner (Reproducible 4F)
- computers or tablets with internet access
- writer's notebooks or Google Docs

Driving Question: How do we persuade the public that a particular fruit or vegetable's health benefits make it the most nutritious food?

Critical Questions: What is a persuasive speech, and how do we write one?

(Available online; see page 7.)

Warm-Up: Using the links provided in Materials, have students listen again to the sample speeches about onions and mangoes. This time, ask them to focus specifically on the introductions. Have them pay close attention to the thesis statement and give a stop signal when they have heard it. When students signal to stop, pause the speech and write the thesis statement on the board. Read the thesis statement aloud, and have students identify the subject, the three topics of the body paragraphs, and the point the author is trying to make.

Teaching Steps

1. Display the Thesis Statement Planner on the board. Then model how to write a thesis statement for your teacher research. (See Teacher Model for Thesis Statement below.)

Teacher Model for Thesis Statement

Remember that when we write a research paper, the thesis statement includes the subject or main idea, the topics of the three body paragraphs, and the point you are trying to make in your paper. A thesis statement in a persuasive paper does the exact same thing, but the point includes your position or purpose—that you are the most nutritious food!

The subject of my paper is okra. Since I am trying to convince voters that okra is the most nutritious food, I am going to include that on my Thesis Statement Planner as my point. Now, I have to figure out how to list the topics of my three body paragraphs. When I was grouping my facts, I found common health benefits in disease prevention, medication, and ridding the body of waste. These ideas are the focus of my three body paragraphs, so I am going to list these on my Thesis Statement Planner as well. I now have all the pieces I need to create my thesis statement: *Okra is the most nutritious food because when you eat it, it prevents diseases, acts as medication, and rids the body of waste.*

That's how I write a thesis statement. But now I must change it to reflect Oakley the Outstanding Okra's point of view. Because I'm writing as Oakley, I must use the pronoun *I*, so this is how I will rewrite it: *I, Oakley the Outstanding Okra, am the most nutritious food because when you eat me, I help prevent diseases, act as medication, and rid the body of wastes.*

2. Distribute students' 4-Pocket Research Organizers and copies of the Thesis Statement Planner. Have students begin writing their own thesis statements.

3. After completing their thesis statements, have students share their statements with a partner. As students share, walk around and conference as needed.

4. Once everyone has shared and revised their thesis statements as needed, have students return to their seats.

5. Next, model writing the introduction. Think aloud about the different types of hooks (e.g., uses a quotation, asks a question, tells a story), and which one might work best for your persuasive speech. (See Teacher Model for Introduction, next page.)

Teacher Model for Introduction

I have the hard part of the introduction—the thesis statement—completed: *I, Oakley the Outstanding Okra, am the most nutritious food because when you eat me, I help prevent diseases, act as medication, and rid the body of wastes.*

Because I am writing a speech, I should probably start by greeting my audience and letting them know who I am: *Hello, I am Oakley the Outstanding Okra.*

Next, I probably want to describe who I am and what I look like. I'm a spiky, green thing . . . hmm. How about this? *You might not recognize me in my natural emerald, spiky-finger shape. Most people see me when I am sliced into my signature star shape and then fried, boiled, or pickled.*

I might need to put a specific fact in here to sound more important. I know okra is a low-calorie food—well, not when it's fried, but otherwise, it is low in calories: *One (non-fried) serving of me is healthy and tasty, for I am a fat- and cholesterol-free food that contains only 30 calories.*

It's sounding better, don't you think? I need a quote or an expert opinion to show I am worthy. Looking through my "Other" pocket, I see a fact slip that says the University of Illinois studied okra and classified it as a "powerhouse of valuable nutrients." I definitely want to include that! It makes me think of a superhero! *According to the University of Illinois, I am a "powerhouse of valuable nutrients."*

Let's go back and reread all my sentences and try to put them together.

Model Introduction

Hello, I am Oakley the Outstanding Okra. According to the University of Illinois, I am a "powerhouse of valuable nutrients." That means I'm a highly nutritious food. You might not recognize me in my natural emerald, spiky-finger shape. Most people see me when I am sliced into my signature star shape and then fried, boiled, or pickled. One (non-fried) serving of me is healthy and tasty, for I am a fat- and cholesterol-free food that contains only 30 calories. I, Oakley the Outstanding Okra, am the most nutritious food, because when you eat me, I help prevent diseases, act as medication, and rid the body of wastes.

6. Before students begin writing their own introduction, review what an introduction needs: a hook, transition sentence(s), and a thesis statement. Pass out copies of the Speech Introduction Planner. While students fill in their planners, circulate around the class to assist and confer as necessary.

7. After students have filled out their Speech Introduction Planners, have them compose their introductions in their writer's notebooks or on their Google Docs with the body paragraphs.

TIP As students write, remind them that they can use the additional facts in the "Other" pocket in their introduction.

Wrap-Up: Pair up students to share their introductions. As they listen to each other, they should make sure their partner's introduction has a greeting, transition sentence with credibility boost, description of the food, and a thesis statement.

LESSON 6: Writing Conclusions

Estimated Teaching Time: One 45-minute class period

Materials
- speech examples
  - Onion: https://bit.ly/2qoGdl4
  - Mango: https://bit.ly/2s2ziyE
- classroom projection system
- copies of Speech Conclusion Planner (Reproducible 4G)
- students' 4-Pocket Research Organizers
- computers or tablets with internet access
- writer's notebooks or Google Dogs

Driving Question: How do we persuade the public that a particular fruit or vegetable's health benefits make it the most nutritious food?

Critical Questions: What is a persuasive speech, and how do we write one?

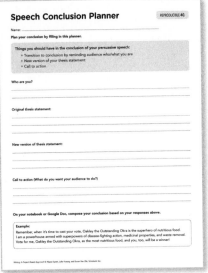

(Available online; see page 7.)

Warm-Up: Start today's lesson by announcing: *Today, we're going to listen to the onion and mango speeches again. This time, I want you to pay close attention to the conclusions. Your mission is to evaluate their effectiveness.* View the videos as a class. After listening to both speeches, ask students how they would rate the speeches, based on what they know about conclusions. Review the three parts of a conclusion: restatement of the thesis, summary of the reasons that support the thesis, and call to action.

Teaching Steps
1. Model how to write the conclusion. First, think aloud about different types of conclusions and which one will work best in your persuasive speech—a "call to action," since students will be voting for the most nutritious food. Use the Speech Conclusion Planner to model writing your conclusion paragraph for the students. (See Teacher Model for Conclusion, next page.)

2. Distribute students' 4-Pocket Research Organizers and copies of the Speech Conclusion Planner. Have students fill out the planner for their chosen food. Walk around and conference with individuals as needed.

3. Allow time for students to draft their conclusions in their writer's notebooks or on their Google Docs.

Wrap-Up: Divide the class into groups of three or four, and have students share their conclusions with one another. After each student shares, direct group members to summarize what the person said. Tell students that if others do not hear what they want the audience to remember, they will need to revise their conclusion.

Teacher Model for Conclusion

As important as your introduction is for grabbing the audience's attention, the conclusion is twice as important because it is the last thing your audience hears from you. The conclusion is where you'll insert your takeaway message: What do you want the audience to remember after you've finished speaking? You want them to vote for your food!

Here's my original thesis statement: *I, Oakley the Outstanding Okra, am the most nutritious food because when you eat me, I help prevent diseases, act as medication, and rid the body of wastes.* I'll need to rework it for

the conclusion. If I just repeat it, my writing will become boring.

Throughout my paper, I mentioned my superhero powers. I probably should finish with that theme, too. How's this? *I am a powerhouse armed with superpowers of disease-fighting action, medicinal properties, and waste removal.*

I have my point or claim and three reasons. I think I will need to remind my audience to vote for me, so I probably should mention my name. I might even want to say: *Vote for me!*

Model Conclusion

Remember, when it's time to cast your vote, Oakley the Outstanding Okra is the superhero of nutritious food. I am a powerhouse armed with superpowers of disease-fighting action, medicinal properties, and waste removal. Vote for me, Oakley the Outstanding Okra, as the most nutritious food, and you, too, will be a winner!

LESSON 7: Revising and Editing

Estimated Teaching Time: One to two 45-minute class periods

Materials

- teacher's essay (or Okra Sample Essay, Reproducible 4D)
- classroom projection system
- copies of Speech Revision Checklist (Reproducible 4H)
- printed copies of each student's persuasive essay
- red and blue pens
- copies of Speech Editing Checklist (Reproducible 4I)
- computers or tablets with internet access
- writer's notebooks or Google Docs

Driving Question: How do we persuade the public that a particular fruit or vegetable's health benefits make it the most nutritious food?

Critical Questions: What is a persuasive speech, and how do we write one?

Warm-Up: Read your speech/essay (or the Okra Sample Essay) to the class. Ask students where they think the speech could use more voice, or POP (Personality on Paper).

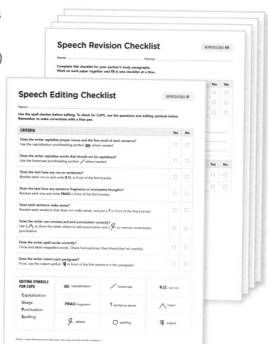

(Available online; see page 7.)

Teacher Model

Today, we're going to revise our papers. As I model how to revise, I want you to pay attention. First, I will read aloud my whole paper. Many times, I catch mistakes when I read it aloud. It's also easier for me to read it to you, just in case you can't read my handwriting. Remember, we're revising, not editing.

After reading my whole paper, I realize that I mention "superhero" and "powers" in my introduction and conclusion, but not in my body paragraphs. I'll start with my first body paragraph: *Numerous people get sick every day with a common cold or even a disease. What if the food you ate gave your body the nutrition it needs to prevent these germs and diseases from invading? Well, look no further! I am full of nutrients and vitamins that have this germ-fighting power!*

I think I'll change *power* to *superpower*. I might want to remind the audience about my name. Maybe I could change it to: *Well, look no further! I, Oakley the Outstanding Okra, am full of nutrients and vitamins that have this germ-fighting superpower!*

Looking at my verbs, I'm not sure they're all vivid. In the following sentence, I need to change the word *get*: *As you can see, okra needs to be added to your diet for your body to get the benefits of vitamin C and folates.* If I get something, I acquire it. I want something stronger, though. How about *reap* instead of *get*? *As you can see, okra needs to be added to your diet for your body to reap the benefits of vitamin C and folates.*

I should also add "like me" after *okra* to reinforce the point of view: *As you can see, okra, like me, needs to be added to your diet for your body to reap the benefits of vitamin C and folates.*

Now, I need to add some adjectives to get the perfect picture in my audience's minds. "Germs" needs to sound worse. I want my audience to realize they need to have okra to "save themselves." When I have a cold, I feel like my body is being taken over by aliens. Perhaps instead of *germs*, I could say *sniffling, runny-nose instigators*.

Now to add a little POP. Perhaps alliteration would help strengthen my writing. I used the word *disease*. I could use an adjective that starts with a *d*. Diseases are destructive. I know my friend with cancer was in a wheelchair because her legs were too weak to walk. It was debilitating. That's it! *Debilitating diseases*. Now, I will reread my paragraph to see if it flows better and is stronger.

Model Body Paragraph 1

Numerous people get sick every day with a common cold or even a disease. What if the food you ate gave your body the nutrition it needs to prevent these sniffling, runny-nose instigators or debilitating diseases from attacking? Well, look no further! I, Oakley the Outstanding Okra, am full of nutrients and vitamins that have this germ-fighting superpower! One cup of me contains 22 percent of the recommended daily allowance of natural folates. Folates (when in their natural state) decrease cancer risks, according to a study conducted by Medical News Today. Okra—that's me—also boosts immune systems and prevents colds, because it contains 36 percent of the recommended daily allowance of vitamin C. Vitamin C fights off radicals (also known as germs) by creating more white blood cells. As you can see, okra, like me, needs to be added to your diet for your body to reap the benefits of vitamin C and folates.

Teaching Steps

1. Begin modeling how to revise your essay/speech. Include your thoughts and opinions, as well as student input, to revise the paper. (See Teacher Model, page 80.)

2. Hand out copies of the Speech Revision Checklist and students' papers. Have students work in pairs to revise their paragraphs. Remind them to focus on only one paper at a time and to note the revisions on the organizer AND on their printed copy of the speech. While students work with their partners, circulate among the class to conference with individuals and add input to student paragraphs.

3. After both partners have completed their revisions, have them make the revisions on their Google Docs or writer's notebooks.

4. Upon completing individual revisions, distribute copies of the Speech Editing Checklist and have students return to work with their partners. Using the checklist, students should peer-edit their papers.

5. After completing the Editing Checklist for each partner's campaign speech, students should make necessary changes within their Google Docs or writer's notebooks.

Wrap-Up: Have students use a "whisper phone" to read aloud their revised campaign speeches. They should rate their work using the following categories: voice, POP, details, reasons and evidence, flow, and persuasive language. Then, have students reflect on whether or not they need to make additional changes to improve the overall quality and impact of their speech. Explain to them that over the next few days they are going to record their campaign speeches, so any additional changes they want to make must be completed by the next class.

LESSON 8: Making Speeches Come to Life

Estimated Teaching Time: One 45-minute class period, plus one week for recording

Before You Start: Prior to starting this lesson, acquaint yourself with Blabberize (blabberize. com) or a similar recording site so that you can guide students as they animate their drawings and record their voices. (Blabberize has a mobile app, but the desktop version is more user friendly.) You can watch a tutorial on YouTube at https://youtu. be/FEtUu1r8Pe4 or follow the steps in How to Use Blabberize (Reproducible 4J).

Materials

- copies of How to Use Blabberize (Reproducible 4J)
- students' drawings and essays/speeches
- computers with internet access
- quiet area for recording
- copies of Audience Viewing Note Sheet (Reproducible 4K)
- copies of Persuasive Speech Rubric (Reproducible 4L)

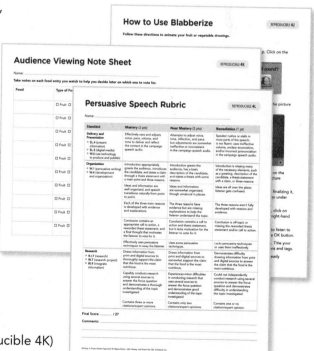

(Available online; see page 7.)

Driving Question: How do we persuade the public that a particular fruit or vegetable's health benefits make it the most nutritious food?

Critical Question: How do we integrate persuasive techniques with factual information to influence an audience's vote?

Warm-Up: Write a sentence for students to read, such as: *"I, Oakley the Outstanding Okra, am full of nutrients and vitamins that have this germ-fighting superpower!"* Ask them to read the sentence in some of the following ways:

- in a toddler's voice
- in a whisper
- with hiccups
- with emphasis on every other word
- getting louder with each word
- getting softer with each word
- with a fun accent
- as a 100-year-old person

Discuss voice qualities, such as volume and inflection, to help them prepare to record their speeches.

Teaching Steps

1. Announce to students that today is recording day! To alleviate jitters, tell them they are going to practice reading their campaign speeches to get the effects they want.

2. Model different ways to read your teacher speech (or Okra speech)—by changing your voice, pausing for dramatic effect, getting louder and quieter, and so on.

Recording a speech on Blabberize

3. Distribute copies of How to Use Blabberize along with students' final speeches. Have them follow the steps to record their speeches on the site. Prior to recording each speech, you must upload the image that corresponds with the speech.

Wrap-Up: After everyone has finished recording their campaign speeches, watch each entry as a class. Distribute copies of the Audience Viewing Note Sheet and have students fill it out to become informed citizens at the voting polls. While students take notes, grade the campaign speeches using the Persuasive Speech Rubric. Once everyone has watched all speeches, conduct an anonymous election and reward the winner with a victory speech and pageant-style ribbon.

The winner of Most Nutritious Food

TIP We have found that recording the speeches almost always takes longer than expected. Once students have practiced reading aloud their speeches, continue with your normal lessons while you send out one student at a time to record his or her voice in the hallway or other quiet space. Depending on your class, internet/server connectivity, and schedules, allot a week to record everyone's speeches. After each recording, you can create a QR code for students to later scan so they can view each campaign speech.

PRODUCING PODCASTS TO ADDRESS SCHOOLWIDE ISSUES

In this project, students engage in the process of solving a school-related problem. First, they identify and describe a problem and discuss why it exists. Then they work in teams to investigate the problem by interviewing experts, conducting surveys, doing research, and more. Because the goal is to help students generate solutions, they create podcasts to broadcast their ideas to other classes and to stimulate interest in forming teams designed to implement solutions to each problem. (Our fifth graders constantly complained about having one less recess than other grade levels, so we investigated this issue to model the steps involved in solving a problem.)

Project-Based Learning Framework

Challenging Problem or Question

Students investigate this driving question: *How do we solve school-related problems?* As teachers, we often hear students voice their complaints about school—excessive cafeteria noise, not enough recess, too much homework, and so on. This project-based learning unit gives students a pathway to investigate a school problem through research, interviews, surveys, and experience. The driving question sets the purpose for learning and encourages students to explore what they can do about their complaints or concerns. As they work through the process of answering this question, they acquire a depth of knowledge and understanding they can use in future learning and, more important, in life.

Sustained Inquiry

To address the driving question, both students and teachers brainstorm problems and concerns related to school. From the list they generate, students choose a problem to research and develop solutions. Students feel engaged because they are working toward finding solutions to a problem that matters to them. As students investigate the problem, they gather information from interviews with an expert (a primary source, such as the principal or someone from the district office), survey the student body, conduct research, and more. They consider the causes of the problem, which experts to consult, costs involved, a plan of action, obstacles that might occur, and possible solutions. Questions requiring research and investigation include the following:

- What is a specific problem at school we would like to solve?
- Who within the school or district can we consult with to help investigate the problem?
- What should we ask in our interview or survey to gather useful data and information that can help us solve our problem?
- How do we analyze the results of our research, surveys, and interviews?
- How do we generate a solution based on our research and data?
- How do we create a podcast to communicate potential solutions to a problem?

Authenticity

This project is authentic because students develop solutions to problems that they feel passionate about. They use real-world strategies, such as surveys, interviews, and persuasive techniques, to investigate their problems and generate potential solutions. To encourage other classes to join solution teams, students broadcast their ideas via podcasts.

Student Voice and Choice

Students maintain complete autonomy over generating topics, forming problem–solution teams, deciding the path of investigation, and weighing different solutions. Although planners, organizers, rubrics, and conferences guide students' work, each team determines how to create a podcast to encourage other students to join in a schoolwide effort to solve the problem.

Reflection

When solving problems, we often have to abandon our original thought process and take a different path toward a solution. Metacognition and reflection help students monitor their progress and enable them to modify the strategies they use to solve their problem. When conferring with groups, it helps to ask questions to aid students' understanding of what strategies to apply, what works, and what does not work. Throughout this project, students reflect on the process with the following questions:

- How do we evaluate resources to identify a problem?
- How do we access the people or resources we need to help develop solutions to a problem?
- How do we generate data to create realistic solutions?
- How do we share solution ideas with a wider audience?

Critique and Revision

During the problem–solution project, students receive constant feedback from their team members and teachers through comments on Google Docs. Google Docs allows team members and teachers to read and critique word choice, ideas, and voice in the podcast scripts. Based on this feedback, students make changes to their work.

Public Products

Throughout the unit, students are engaged in learning and are motivated to come up with potential solutions to their problems. The purpose of the podcast is to generate interest in other classes to help solve schoolwide issues. Students in these classes can be invited to join solution teams to help implement proposed solutions. While not all of the problems identified may be solved, students learn that even 10- and 11-year-olds are capable of investigating and developing solutions to problems.

LESSON 1: Identifying Problems

Estimated Teaching Time: One 45-minute class period

Materials

- 2 different-size hula hoops
- Problem Sorting Cards (Reproducible 5A), cut apart
- *What Do You Do With a Problem?* by Kobi Yamada
- writer's notebooks
- chart paper or whiteboard
- copies of Problems I'm Most Passionate About (Reproducible 5B)

Driving Question: How do we solve school-related problems?

Critical Question: What is a specific problem at school we would like to solve?

Warm-Up: Lay the two hula hoops in the middle of the floor so that the smaller one is inside the larger one, like concentric circles. With the class, discuss how in life we are often confronted with situations. Some situations are in our control; other times, we have no control over them. Distribute the Problem Sorting Cards to students. Have students work in pairs to discuss whether they have control or no control over the problem written on their card. If they determine they have control over the problem, tell them to place the card in the center of the smaller hula hoop. If they do not have control, direct students to place the card between the small and large hoops. As a class, observe where students place the cards and ask the class whether they agree with each placement.

(Available online; see page 7.)

Students sort problem cards according to whether or not we have control over the problems.

Teaching Steps

1. Read aloud the book *What Do You Do With a Problem?* by Kobi Yamada. This book encourages students to look closely at problems and discover the possibilities they can hold.

2. In their writer's notebooks, have students make a list of problems they have noticed in school. Give them approximately five minutes to free-write. (Sample problems may include: wanting more recess time; excessive noise in the lunchroom; unfair punishment, as when the whole class suffers the consequences for the actions of a few.)

3. Divide the class in half and form two concentric circles of students. Have those in the inside circle face those in the outside circle. Invite students to take turns sharing two problems they have

identified, along with what they know about the causes and effects of the problem. As they do this, allow students to add to their lists in their notebooks. Then have students in the outside circle rotate to their right and repeat the process with a new person. Continue until everyone has shared with every student in the other circle.

4. After students have shared problems with one another, invite them to come together to create a class chart of the problems they identified.

5. Review the list of problems as a class, identifying and crossing out those that are beyond their control, such as shortening the school year or eliminating gym (these are impacted by state law).

Problems identified by our fifth graders

Our Experience: Flipgrid is an app and web-based platform that allows students to post and discuss their thoughts or reflections in 90 seconds or less. We used Flipgrid to identify and share about problems in our school. Our students' personalities shone through as they spoke about what they'd like to change in the school. They also enjoyed viewing and commenting on classmates' videos. It was an amazing, engaging way for them to build on one another's ideas.

Wrap-Up: Explain to students that they will form problem-solving teams to generate possible solutions to problems on the class list. To determine these teams, distribute copies of Problems I'm Most Passionate About and instruct students to list three issues they would like to investigate and solve, and then tell them to give their lists to you. Alternatively, you can have a volunteer type in the list of potential problems on a Google form and have students mark their top three choices on this form.

LESSON 2: Consulting Others for Help

Estimated Teaching Time: One 45-minute class period

Before You Start: Prior to class, review students' completed Problems I'm Most Passionate About and form problem–solution teams based on what problems students want to pursue, as well as their personalities and abilities. We have found that teams of three work best, because there is always a deciding vote.

Materials
- for each group of 3 or 4 students:
  - vinyl record
  - straight pin
  - sheet of paper
  - pencil
  - transparent tape

- copies of Record Problem Reflection Sheet (Reproducible 5C)
- video clip of Mr. Wizard: https://youtu.be/HJa6Ik6xmiU
- classroom projection system
- copies of Step #1: Describing the Problem (Reproducible 5D)
- computers or devices with internet access
- access to Google Drive for each team (optional)

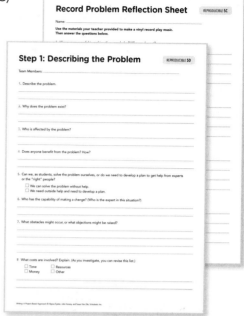

(Available online; see page 7.)

Driving Question: How do we solve school-related problems?

Critical Questions

- When trying to solve a problem, to whom can we turn for help?
- Who within the school or district can we consult with to help investigate the problem?

Warm-Up: Divide the class into groups of three or four students (different from the problem–solution teams). Tell students that you will present them with a problem. Give each group a vinyl record, straight pin, paper, pencil, and tape. If necessary, explain what a vinyl record is and how it plays music. Then direct students to use the materials you gave them to make the record play music. Allow them five minutes to explore and experiment with the materials. Afterward, pass out copies of the Record Problem Reflection Sheet and have students fill it out.

Teaching Steps

1. Ask students: *Do you think it would have been easier to solve this problem if you had been able to consult an expert?* After a brief discussion, show the class the Mr. Wizard video clip (link on Materials), which demonstrates how to use the same materials to play a record.

Students try to make a record player.

2. As a class, discuss how consulting an expert can be useful in solving a problem. Emphasize how helpful experts can be!

3. Now that they have an expert's instructions, allow the groups to make another attempt at making the record play. Afterward, discuss whether the video helped. Explain that as students work on solving the problems they identified in the previous lesson, they may need to consult experts.

4. Tell students: *In our last class, we listed things that bothered or concerned us in our school. Before you left, you chose three problems you were passionate about. Today, you will meet with others who share the same passion about a problem as you do. Before we form our teams, let's go over the first step of problem-solving. I will use the problem of limited recess to model the process your teams will use.*

5. Display Step 1: Describing the Problem on the board. As you discuss how to address the issue of recess, ask students for input and suggestions to help you complete the form. (See Sample Class Discussion, page 88.)

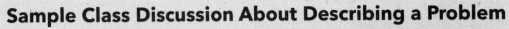

Sample Class Discussion About Describing a Problem

Teacher: Recess time appears on our list of school problems. What do you mean by this?

Student: Kindergarten through fourth grade have two recesses, while fifth grade has only one recess and a study hall. We would like to have two recesses, because this is our last year in elementary school, and there's no recess in middle school.

Teacher: Why do you think this problem exists?

Students:
- Maybe the teachers and principal think we need a study hall instead of recess because we have more homework.
- Since we have study hall, there might not be enough time in the school day for a second recess.
- There may not be enough adults to cover recess duty.

Teacher: Who is affected by less recess time?

Student: It affects us! We need a brain break. If we have a break between social studies and math, we can focus better in math class. Also, you would have more time to set up for math class while we play.

Teacher: Who benefits because fifth graders do not have a second recess, and how do they benefit?

Students:
- Teachers benefit because they have more time to teach us.
- Some kids who need extra help benefit because they can get it during study hall.

Teacher: Can you, as students, solve this problem, or will you need help?

Student: We need help and permission.

Teacher: Who could help you?

Student: Our principal, teachers, parents, and the bosses (administrators) can help us make a change.

Teacher: What obstacles might occur?

Students:
- Scheduling a second recess might be difficult.
- Convincing the principal to replace study hall with recess could be hard.

Teacher: What costs are involved? Remember, "cost" doesn't always mean money. How might time be a factor?

Student: Adding a second recess reduces class time.

Teacher: Will adding a second recess cost money?

Student: Yes, recess aides will need to stay at school longer and be paid for supervising us.

Teacher: What other resources are involved if we add another recess?

Students:
- We might lose more balls and playground equipment because we have more time to play. These would have to be replaced.
- Custodians would have to clean the playground more often, so they would have more work.

Teacher: Can you think of any other costs involved if we add another recess?

Student: We might have more playground accidents since we have more time outside. This gives the nurse more work.

Teacher: You have done a great job thinking about the recess problem and describing it. You are now ready to talk about the problem you chose yesterday.

6. Announce the different problem–solution teams. Then distribute a copy of Step 1: Describing the Problem to each student (or have each team access a shared copy of the document in their Google Drive). Give teams 10 to 15 minutes to work together to complete the form.

Wrap-Up: Say to students: *We started class by trying to figure out how to play a record. To successfully solve this problem, we had to consult an expert—Mr. Wizard. As we end class, I would like each team to briefly describe the problem they're trying to solve and suggest a possible expert with whom they can consult.* Invite each team to share their problem with the class.

> **TIP** Using Google Docs helps students in each team collaborate on a single document. Also, when class time is at a premium, teachers and students can use the comment feature to conference electronically.

LESSON 3: Investigating the Problem

Estimated Teaching Time: One 45-minute class period, plus a week for investigation

Materials

- classroom projection system
- computers or tablets with internet access
- students' completed Step 1: Describing the Problem (from Lesson 2)
- copies of Step 2: Investigating the Problem (Reproducible 5E)
- access to Google Drive for each team (optional)
- copies of Step 3: Analyzing the Results of the Investigation (Reproducible 5F)
- writer's notebooks

Driving Question: How do we solve school-related problems?

Critical Questions

- Who within the school or district can we consult with to help investigate the problem?
- What should we ask in our interview or survey to gather useful data and information that can help us solve our problem?
- Besides interviews and surveys, what other methods can we use to investigate our problem?

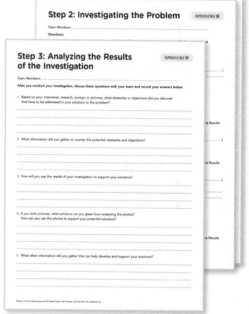

(Available online; see page 7.)

Warm-Up: Return students' completed Step 1: Describing the Problem handouts and tell problem–solution teams to review their descriptions of their problems. Ask them to star two questions/sections where they need additional information or help. Pair two different problem–solution teams. First, have each team share its description of the problem. Then, ask listeners to provide specific suggestions for improving the description. Next, have teams offer suggestions and ideas for the two areas each one starred. Direct teams to record relevant information.

Teaching Steps

1. As a whole class, explore how to investigate a problem. Continue to use the problem of limited recess time and the Sample Class Discussion below to acquaint students with different strategies for exploring a problem.

Sample Class Discussion About Investigating a Problem

Teacher: How many of you would like a second recess? (*All hands go up.*) Well, if this is something you really want, we can build a case for why you deserve it. We have some options on how to investigate this problem. We could do interviews, research, surveys, or even take pictures or videos to demonstrate the need. Any ideas about how you could investigate the problem?

Student: When I ask my parents for something, I think about all the reasons they'll say no first.

Teacher: Interesting! Let's explore this a bit more. In your teams, take a minute to discuss the reasons we might be told that we cannot have a second recess.

Students:
- Recess takes away class time.
- You need time to do in-class assignments and homework.
- You already have one recess.
- Next year, you won't have recess, so we're preparing you for this.
- You're older, so you can focus longer and don't need recess.

Teacher: What should we do with the "no" reasons now?

Student: Think of a reason each "no" would not be true.

Teacher: So, how might we counter this argument: "You're older, so you can focus longer"?

Student: We could research what attention spans are for each grade level.

Teacher: Research is a great way to investigate. What else could we research?

Student: Reasons recess is good for fifth graders.

Teacher: How else might we investigate this problem?

Students:
- We could find out who made the decision to eliminate a second recess and why.
- We could interview the principal or teacher to see if a second recess could be added again.
- What if we did a video to show how unfocused we are during math?
- How about asking the fifth-grade teachers if they'd be willing to supervise us?

Teacher: What is it called when we ask people for information or opinions about a topic?

Students:
- Interview
- Poll
- Survey

Teacher: A survey allows us to document information and opinions from multiple people. Therefore, we could survey the teachers and students to see if there is a need or desire for additional recess time.

2. Tell students: *We mentioned two important ideas when we were discussing the recess problem. First, someone suggested interviewing the principal or teacher to learn more. Second, someone mentioned using a survey to collect data about people's opinions related to the problem. To help you begin your investigations, let's take a look at how to conduct an interview.*

3. Ask: *What is an interview?* (a meeting at which someone is asked questions) Write its definition on the whiteboard.

4. Have students imagine they are going to interview the principal to address the problem of limited recess time. To help them determine what questions to ask, first have them state the purpose for interviewing the principal and what they hope to achieve. As students respond, jot down their ideas on the board and use these ideas to reach consensus on a goal statement. For example, a goal for the interview might be to determine what steps need to be taken to get a second recess.

5. Once students identify the goal for interviewing the principal, brainstorm questions related to attaining the goal. Potential questions could include:

   - Why do fifth graders have fewer recesses than other grade levels? (Knowing why can help students identify obstacles they need to overcome to achieve their goal.)
   - For fifth graders to have the opportunity for a second recess, what needs to happen? (This directly addresses the goal and helps students know what they have to do to attain it.)
   - What effects do you think reduced recess time has on fifth graders? (This could yield information about why a second recess is necessary, which supports the implementation of steps needed to secure one.)

6. Say: *Now that you know what an interview entails and how it can support your investigation of the problem, let's look at the difference between an interview and a survey. What is a survey?* Before they respond, have students think about surveys they have completed. Guide them to discover that a survey is a way to collect data from a group of people to gain information and insights on various topics. Emphasize that because surveys have a variety of purposes, the goal of the survey needs to be clear before designing one.

   > **TIP** As students generate the class interview questions, constantly ask how each question relates to the goal. This reinforces the thought process they need to use when they begin to generate their own interview questions.

7. Next, ask students how an interview differs from a survey. List their responses on the board. Responses might include:

   - surveys involve more people
   - interviews are more open-ended, and you can ask follow-up questions
   - surveys can have different formats

8. Once students understand the difference between an interview and a survey, ask them to think about a purpose for conducting a survey to address the recess problem. Demonstrate how to develop some survey questions. Use the Sample Class Discussion on page 92 to guide the process.

9. Pair up students. Ask partners to create another question for the recess survey. Have partners share their question with the class. Write each question on the board and ask the class if it fits the purpose of the survey. If the question does not support the purpose, delete it. If the question is valid, ask students to generate multiple-choice responses for it.

Sample Class Discussion About Conducting a Survey

Teacher: Now that we know the difference between an interview and a survey, let's identify our purpose for using a survey. What is the purpose for creating a survey to address the problem of limited recess time?

Student: To show that kids need recess.

Teacher: Why would we want to do this? How does it relate to our problem?

Student: Proving kids need recess could help us replace study hall with recess.

Teacher: Great! So the purpose of our survey is to prove that recess is more beneficial than study hall and should replace it. (*Write the purpose on the board*.) Now that we have the purpose for our survey, what kinds of questions will we need to ask to support our purpose?

Student: We could ask students how they use study-hall time.

Teacher: Why?

Student: If kids do not do homework or ask a teacher for help, then what's the point of study hall? It could be eliminated and replaced with recess.

Teacher: Okay, let's try to come up with a survey question related to this idea.

Student: We could ask, "How do you use your study-hall time?"

Teacher: This question might be too broad because multiple-choice responses might include such things as:

- I do homework.
- I ask a teacher for help.
- I doodle.

We need to narrow down the question to fit our purpose. If we ask, "How often do you do homework during study hall," responses might be:

- I frequently do homework.
- I sometimes do homework.
- I rarely do homework.

Narrowing the question helps us discover whether students need the study hall. If many rarely do homework, this could support the idea that study hall can be eliminated and replaced with recess. What is a second question we might ask?

Student: We could ask students how often they ask a teacher for help during study hall.

Teacher: How does this relate to our purpose?

Student: If the majority of students rarely ask for help, it gives us another reason to get rid of study hall.

Teacher: Exactly!

10. Distribute copies of Step 2: Investigating the Problem (or upload the document, share it with problem–solution teams, and have students access it from their Google Drives). Review the directions with students and emphasize that teams should choose the strategy that works best for their problem. For instance, state that interviewing the principal about the recess problem and conducting research might be better options than a survey because they will yield more information.

11. Provide time during the following week for students to conduct surveys, interview experts, and gather research. Each team member should be in charge of at least one option: interview, research, survey, pictures, or other. If the research is extensive, students can divide the responsibility among team members.

12. Circulate and check in with each team every day. Have copies of Step 3: Analyzing the Results of the Investigation available for students to complete as they finish their investigations (or have students use the shared document on Google Drive).

Wrap-Up: Ask students to think about the process of investigating a problem. In their writer's notebooks, have them do a 3-2-1 and state three things they learned, two things they found interesting, and one question they still have. Afterward, have them share their responses with a partner.

> **TIP** As the problem–solution teams conduct their investigations, make sure to constantly circulate and conference with each team. This keeps them focused and helps them develop stronger interview, research, and survey questions. If students are using Google Drive, you can comment on their work electronically after school if you run out of time to conference in class.

LESSON 4: Proposing Solutions

Estimated Teaching Time: One 45-minute class period

Materials
- *Dog Breath: The Horrible Trouble With Hally Tosis* by Dav Pilkey
- students' interviews, research, survey, etc., from their investigations (from Lesson 3)
- students' completed Step 3: Analyzing the Results of the Investigation (from Lesson 3)
- computers or tablets with internet access
- classroom projection system
- copies of Step 4: Proposing Solutions (Reproducible 5G)
- sticky notes

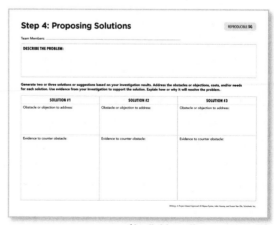

(Available online; see page 7.)

Driving Question: How do we solve school-related problems?

Critical Questions

- How do we analyze the results of our research, surveys, and interviews?
- How do we generate a solution based on our research and data?

Warm-Up: Read aloud the picture book *Dog Breath* by Dav Pilkey. This is a humorous picture book about a dog named Hally Tosis, who has very bad breath. The family tries several solutions to get rid of their dog's problem. After reading the story, have students summarize the ways in which the family tried to solve their problem. Was there one solution in the end that worked?

Teaching Steps

1. Tell students: *Like the family in our story, we need to begin working toward possible solutions to the problems we investigated. So far, we have identified each problem and used research, interviews, surveys, and other methods to investigate it. What do we do now? How do we use our information to create possible solutions?*

2. Instruct problem–solution teams to collect all of the information they have gathered during their investigations and make sure each team member has access to it.

3. Tell students to take out their Step 3: Analyzing the Results of the Investigation handout or open the shared Google Doc. Have students look at their responses to question 1 regarding obstacles or objections they encountered. Before students review their findings, share your response to the first question. Use the Teacher Think-Aloud below about the limited-recess problem to guide you.

Teacher Think-Aloud About Obstacles

The first obstacle I found to adding another recess to the school day is time. Currently, there is not enough time in the school day to add a second recess.

When I interviewed the principal, she said the district does not have enough money to pay aides to supervise a second recess, so money is a second obstacle.

Even though I do not have this written in my response to Question 1, I discovered a third obstacle when I looked over my notes. The principal kept saying that fifth graders need more instructional time because of the challenging curriculum and testing demands. I am going to add that to my planner and make sure I have information I can use to overcome this obstacle.

4. Allow 5 to 10 minutes for teams to review their responses to question 1 of the Step 3 handout and change or add any information. Check in with each team as they work.

5. Instruct teams to reread their responses to the remaining questions on the handout. As they read, tell them to look for information to counter the obstacles they identified in question 1. For example, note that training volunteers for recess duty could help counter the obstacle of not being able to pay aides to supervise a second recess. Encourage students to add more ideas and information to their Step 3 handout. Be available for teams to consult with you as they analyze their data.

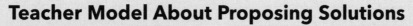

Teacher Model About Proposing Solutions

Now that I have investigated the recess problem, I can describe it in a little more detail. The problem is that fifth graders have one less recess than other grade levels. I know there are three main reasons for the problem: no time for a second recess, no money to pay aides to supervise students, and fifth graders need more instructional time because of testing and curriculum demands. (Write these ideas under "Describe the Problem" on the organizer.)

DESCRIBE THE PROBLEM:

Fifth graders have one less recess than other grade levels. Three reasons for this problem exist: There is no time for a second recess, no money to pay aides to supervise students, and fifth graders need more instructional time because of testing and curriculum demands.

In analyzing my results, the first obstacle I identified is time. Under Solution #1 where it says, "Obstacle or objection to address," I am going to write: *No time for a second recess.*

Now, I need to provide evidence to counter this objection. From my investigation, I discovered that taking away three minutes of instructional time from each fifth-grade class adds 15 minutes to the schedule. I'm going to write this evidence in the second box under Solution #1.

From my interview with the principal, I found out she is concerned about taking away any instructional time, so I have to prove that the time we want to take away will benefit students and help them learn. I researched the benefits of recess and discovered it improves memory, helps kids burn energy to improve focus, and develops the brain. I'll add these to my organizer.

I also found a quote from the American Academy of Pediatrics that says, "Play is essential to children's development." Using experts to show kids need recess might also strengthen my proposed solution, so I'll add this to my organizer.

I have some other benefits in my research notes, such as recess teaches kids to socialize, take turns, and so on, but these do not seem to belong here, so I will not include them.

SOLUTION #1

Obstacle or objection to address:

No time for a second recess

Evidence to counter obstacle:

- Take away 3 minutes of instructional time from each class to add 15 minutes of recess
- Research shows second recess improves memory, helps kids burn energy to improve focus, and develops the brain.
- The American Academy of Pediatrics says, "Play is essential to children's development."

---

6. After students have enough time to review their analysis, display Step 4: Proposing Solutions on the whiteboard and distribute copies to students. Using the limited-recess time problem, think aloud to describe the process of using the information collected from investigating the problem to generate potential solutions. (See Teacher Model, page 95.)

7. After modeling the thought process for proposing solutions, provide time for students to complete their organizers.

> **TIPS** Save your model of Step 4: Proposing Solutions (see Teacher Model, page 95) and use it to model how to write the podcast script in Lesson 5.
>
> You may want to modify the number of solutions teams generate if it becomes difficult for them to create a third solution. Most groups should be able to develop two viable solutions to their problem.

Wrap-Up: Distribute sticky notes to problem–solution teams and then pair up two different teams. Tell them to exchange their Step 4: Proposing Solutions organizers. Instruct teams to review each other's organizers and use the sticky notes to provide written feedback. (Teams using Google Docs can use the comment feature.) List the following questions on the board to guide students as they evaluate their peers' work:

- How clear is the description of the problem? Are reasons provided to show why the problem exists?
- Are the obstacles the team identified related to the problem? Can you think of additional obstacles the team might face as they work toward a solution?
- How well does the evidence counter each obstacle or objection raised?
- Is more evidence needed? If so, suggest where it is needed and offer suggestions about what kind of information to add.

Direct students to make revisions based on their peers' suggestions.

LESSON 5: Writing the Podcast Script

Estimated Teaching Time: One 45-minute class period

Materials

- chart paper and markers
- 3 different-color sticky notes
- classroom projection system
- students' completed copies of Step 4: Proposing Solutions (from Lesson 4)
- copies of Step 5: Writing the Podcast Script (Reproducible 5H), one per team
- copies of the Teacher Model Podcast Script (Reproducible 5I)
- access to Google Drive for each team (optional)

Driving Question: How do we solve school-related problems?

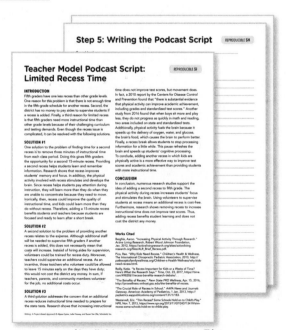

(Available online; see page 7.)

Critical Question: How do we create a podcast to communicate potential solutions to a problem?

Warm-Up: On chart paper, create a three-column chart with the following headers:

- What is a podcast?
- What is the purpose of a podcast?
- What are some examples of podcasts?

Divide the class into random groups of three. (Make sure members of the same problem–solution teams are not grouped together.) Distribute three different-color sticky notes to each group. Assign a specific sticky-note color for each question (e.g., yellow for definition of a podcast, blue for purpose of a podcast, pink for examples) and instruct students to write their responses to the questions on these. Remind groups that podcasts may have more than one purpose. As students generate examples of familiar podcasts, ask them to think about the purpose for each one to help activate their prior knowledge. Provide five minutes for brainstorming.

Afterward, have group members stick their colored notes to the appropriate column on the chart. As a whole class, read and discuss the information collected. Generate a definition for a podcast and write it on the board. Compile a list of the common purposes and examples. List these on the board as well.

Teaching Steps

1. Tell students they are going to use the information from their investigations and Step 4: Proposing Solutions organizer to create a podcast. Explain that the purpose of this podcast is to inform other classes about school-related problems that they've identified and their proposed solutions. Note that the ultimate goal is to have students from other classes join a solution team and devise a plan of action to implement the solutions. Emphasize that presenting the problem and possible solutions is just the first step toward their long-term goal.

2. Explain that before they record their podcasts, they need to write a script to be sure their content is solid. Use the Teacher Model About Proposing Solutions (page 95) to demonstrate how to craft the description of the problem and the first solution for the script.

3. Display a copy of Step 5: Writing the Podcast Script on the whiteboard and use the Teacher Model on the next page as a guide for writing the podcast.

4. After rereading and revising the script, tell students to take out their completed copy of Step 4: Proposing Solutions and place it in front of them. Distribute a copy of Step 5: Writing the Podcast Script to each team (or upload the reproducible to Google Drive and share the document with each problem–solution team).

> **TIP** As you model the script writing, be sure students can see the Step 4: Proposing Solutions organizer you are using to draft the description and solutions. You can enlarge your notes, hang them on the board, and refer to them as you write. If your whiteboard has a dual-screen feature, you can show both the organizer and the podcast script simultaneously.

5. Direct students to use the notes on their Proposing Solutions organizer to write their script as a team. Suggest that while one group member writes or types, the other two can use the organizer to craft sentences and transitions. Have team members rotate the role of writer so that a different student writes each solution.

6. After each solution is drafted, instruct the team to reread it aloud and then revise and edit it.

Teacher Model for Writing a Podcast

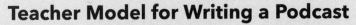

On my Proposing Solutions organizer, I have a good description of my problem that I can use for my podcast introduction: *Fifth graders have one less recess than other grade levels.*

I need to elaborate on my reasons for the problem in the script's introduction. It's a good idea to explain each reason in a separate sentence. I'll start out by saying: *One reason for this problem is that there is not enough time in the fifth-grade schedule for another recess.*

What transition can I use to add my second reason? I can say: *Second, the district has no money to pay aides to supervise students if a recess is added.*

I need another transition to show I'm stating my third and final reason. I can write: *Finally, a third reason for limited recess is that fifth graders need more instructional time than other grade levels because of their challenging curriculum and testing demands.*

Now, I need a clincher sentence to lead into my first solution. Well, even though the problem is difficult, it can still be solved. Maybe I can say: *Even though the recess issue is complicated, it can be resolved with the following solutions.* I think that works. I don't want to get too wordy or flowery since I am writing an informative podcast.

The next step is to use my notes to write Solution #1. I can start with this: *One solution to the problem of finding time for a second recess is to remove three minutes of instructional time from each class period.*

Next, I need to describe what happens as a result of this action. I'll say: *Doing this gives fifth graders the opportunity for a second 15-minute recess.*

Okay. Here is the hard part. I have to show these 15 minutes are more beneficial than the loss of instructional time. What student benefits does a second recess provide? My planner notes suggest that recess helps kids learn and remember information. So, I'll begin with: *Providing a second recess helps students learn and remember information.*

How do I back up this idea? Well, according to my research, recess improves memory, focus, and brain development. I'll make two sentences out of this: *Research shows that recess improves students' memory and focus. In addition, the physical activity involved with recess stimulates and develops the brain.*

Phew! How do I show that adding a second recess will actually improve the quality of instructional time because kids learn more when they can focus and concentrate? I've got it! *Since recess helps students pay attention during instruction, they will learn more than they do when they are unable to concentrate because they need to move.*

I want to emphasize this point since instructional time is so important to the principal. It's really ironic that recess can improve the quality of instructional time. To drive this point home, I'll write: *Ironically, then, recess could improve the quality of instructional time, and kids could learn more than they do without recess.*

I'll wrap up my thoughts with a clincher now. *Therefore, adding a 15-minute recess benefits students and teachers because students are focused and ready to learn after a short break.*

Now, I'll reread what I wrote to see if it makes sense or needs to be revised.

Step 5: Writing the Podcast Script REPRODUCIBLE 5H

INTRODUCTION (Describe the problem.)

Fifth graders have one less recess than other grade levels. One reason for this problem is that there is not enough time in the fifth-grade schedule for another recess. Second, the district has no money to pay aides to supervise students if a recess is added. Finally, a third reason for limited recess is that fifth graders need more instructional time than other grade levels because of their challenging curriculum and testing demands. Even though the recess issue is complicated, it can be resolved with the following solutions.

SOLUTION #1 (Include support and evidence from your research.)

One solution to the problem of finding time for a second recess is to remove three minutes of instructional time from each class period. Doing this gives fifth graders the opportunity for a second 15-minute recess. Providing a second recess helps students learn and remember information. Research shows that recess improves students' memory and focus. In addition, the physical activity involved with recess stimulates and develops the brain. Since recess helps students pay attention during instruction, they will learn more than they do when they are unable to concentrate because they need to move. Ironically, then, recess could improve the quality of instructional time, and kids could learn more than they do without recess. Therefore, adding a 15-minute recess benefits students and teachers because students are focused and ready to learn after a short break.

7. Have team members collaborate to write their conclusion or final thoughts. Place copies of the Teacher Model Podcast Script in a convenient location (or upload it to Google Drive and share it with problem–solution teams) so students can refer to it as they write.

Wrap-Up: Pair up problem–solution teams. As one team reads aloud each segment of its script (the introduction, solutions, and final thoughts), the other team listens carefully and jots down notes about what impresses or confuses them. Require the "sounding board" team to give feedback after each segment is read. Then have teams switch roles.

Each team member should write a part of the script.

TIP Some teams may struggle to ensure that every member does his or her fair share, so circulate regularly to ask each member what he or she has contributed to the writing. If a team has a nonparticipant, help the team solve the problem by asking questions such as, "Have you specifically asked your team member to add a sentence or offer a transition? What kinds of things can you say to be clear about how you want him or her to help? Have you tried assigning him or her the role of writer, sentence generator, or reviewer?"

LESSON 6: Recording the Podcast

Estimated Teaching Time: One 45-minute class period

Before You Start: Choose a device and app for students to record their podcasts, then record your Teacher Model Podcast.

Materials
- copies of Podcast Rubric (Reproducible 5J)
- Student Model Podcast (available online, see page 7)
- device to play the Student Model Podcast
- classroom projection system
- teams' completed Step 5: Writing the Podcast Script (from Lesson 5)
- copies of Step 6: Recording the Podcast (Reproducible 5K)
- device and app to create the podcast (see Tip below)
- shared Google folder titled "Problem–Solution Podcasts" (where students can upload their podcasts)
- writer's notebooks

Driving Question: How do we solve school-related problems?

Critical Question: How do we create a podcast to communicate potential solutions to a problem?

Warm-Up: Direct students to say the phrase "I love you" using different tones. Ask them to say it enthusiastically, casually, sarcastically, or flatly. Discuss the importance of tone when creating a podcast, emphasizing the need to vary it to keep the listener engaged.

(Available online; see page 7.)

TIP We used' iPads and the app Voice Memos to create our podcasts. Depending on the device and app you choose for students to record their podcasts, you may need to modify the directions on Step 6: Recording the Podcast.

Teaching Steps

1. Distribute a copy of the Podcast Rubric to each team. As a class, review the criteria for evaluating the podcast.

2. Tell students that you will play the Student Model Podcast and that they should be prepared to evaluate it. Display a copy of the Podcast Rubric on the whiteboard. As a class, evaluate the student model and have students justify their scores.

3. Direct students to access their podcast scripts.

4. Distribute a copy of Step 6: Recording the Podcast to each team and review the directions.

5. Allow ample time for students to plan, record, test market (receive feedback from peers), revise, and record their podcasts.

Wrap-Up: On their writer's notebooks, have students reflect on the process involved in solving their chosen problem from start to finish. Have students respond to this prompt: *Describe the process for solving a schoolwide problem.* Encourage students to use writing, drawing, flow charts, or a list of steps to convey their understanding. Provide time for them to share their responses with a partner and discuss their ideas as a whole class.

TIP Students tend to be wizards at using podcast apps! Once our students planned how they wanted to record as a group, the recording proceeded quickly. The biggest difficulty was finding a quiet, disruption-free location for recording.

Find a quiet spot for students to record their podcasts.

LESSON 7: Evaluating and Implementing Solutions

Estimated Teaching Time: One 45-minute class period

Materials
- device to access and play students' podcasts
- copies of Step 7: Evaluating the Solutions (Reproducible 5L)

Driving Question: How do we solve school-related problems?

Critical Questions
- How do we evaluate and rate our solutions?
- How do we begin implementing solutions to schoolwide problems?

Warm-Up: Tell the class that as they listen to their peers' podcasts, they are going to decide which team has solutions that could actually be implemented. Discuss what makes an effective solution and list students' ideas on the board. For example, a viable solution needs to be practical, cost effective, and easy to do. Have students refer to this list as they evaluate their peers' solutions.

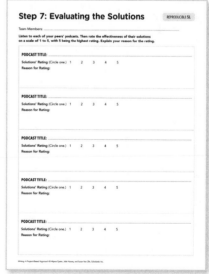

(Available online; see page 7.)

Teaching Steps

1. Distribute copies of Step 7: Evaluating the Solutions and review the directions. Emphasize that students should refer to the class criteria for effective solutions to rate the solutions.

2. Play the podcasts and provide time for students to rate each one.

3. Afterward, direct project–solution teams to meet to discuss their ratings and reach consensus on a solution they think could be implemented.

4. Have each team share its decision with the class and defend its choice. Record the titles of all podcasts on the board and have the class vote on the podcast that offers the most effective solutions.

Wrap-Up: Play the winning podcast and ask students to choose one of the possible solutions to implement. After the class reaches consensus, collectively develop an action plan for implementation. For example, if students choose to solve the problem of limited recess time, their first step may be to go to the principal with their research showing that removing 15 minutes of instructional time and adding a recess may actually help kids learn more. Subsequent steps in the action plan would include such things as securing volunteers to supervise students to reduce costs.

TIP Consider setting up stations and having the problem–solution teams listen to the podcasts on student iPads or other devices. After team members individually rate the podcast, have them rotate to the next one.

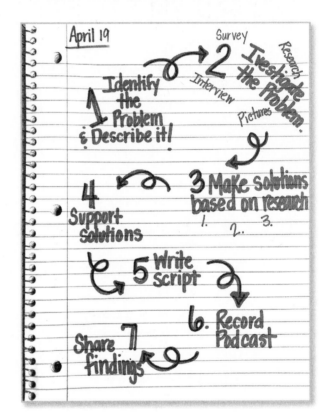

DEVELOPING, DESIGNING, AND MARKETING INVENTIONS AND INNOVATIONS

CHAPTER 6

Our students' interests in inventions and innovations inspired this unit and generated the question: *How do we turn ideas into inventions and innovations?* In addressing this question, students engage in several 21st-century skills used in the workplace. They work in small business teams to brainstorm new product ideas, choose a viable product, conduct research to determine its validity, and investigate the market to see if similar products exist. Each business team then designs a model of their invention/innovation; creates a company name, logo, and business card; conducts surveys; analyzes their data; and generates bar graphs to showcase their results. They create a business proposal and a multimedia presentation to introduce and market their invention/innovation to a real-world audience—a panel of judges.

Without a doubt, this unit demonstrates the transformative power of project-based learning. If we continue to value students' curiosity, and encourage them to collaborate, investigate, communicate, solve problems, and generate meaningful products, our schools will become vibrant, lively places of learning, and our students will be ready for real-world joys and challenges.

Project-Based Learning Framework

Challenging Problem or Question

Students investigate this driving question: *How do we turn our ideas into inventions or innovations?* This question sets the purpose for learning and allows students to use the knowledge they gain to create a model of an invention or innovation and to market it. As students work through the process of answering this question, they acquire a depth of knowledge and understanding that they can use in future learning. Certainly, the critical-thinking, problem-solving, communication, team-building, and technology skills students employ during the unit prepare them to meet the demands of the 21st century.

Sustained Inquiry

To address the driving question, both students and teachers activate their prior knowledge and identify what they need to research and investigate to produce their inventions or innovations.

As students engage in the project, their inquiry is sustained. For example, when designing their invention/innovation, students collaborate, solve problems, and self-manage their time. They continue to use these skills as they draft and revise their business proposals, create their commercials, and design their presentations. Questions requiring research and investigation include:

- How do we use our ideas to develop a product?
- How do we know if our product is viable?
- How do we promote our business?
- How do we write a business proposal?
- What persuasive techniques can we use to enhance our commercial?
- How do we create and present an effective presentation?

Authenticity

The context of the project is authentic because students design and market a product using real-world strategies, such as conducting surveys, writing business proposals, and advertising techniques. Additionally, the task—creating an invention/innovation—and the tools students use to complete the task—such as Google Slides, iPads, and marketing techniques—mirror the real world. Moreover, experts from the community instruct students, teaching them the basic principles of marketing a product.

Student Voice and Choice

Students maintain complete autonomy over the invention/innovation they choose to create. If business teams experience a problem, they solve it themselves. Although planners, organizers, and rubrics guide students' work, each business team determines how to develop their product, proposal, and presentation.

Reflection

Metacognition and reflection help students monitor their progress and enable them to modify the strategies they use to learn. As you confer with various business teams, ask them questions to aid students' understanding of the strategy they apply, what works, and what does not work. Cooperative learning rubrics, journal responses, and final reflection questions are available to assist students with their metacognition.

Critique and Revision

During the unit, students receive constant feedback. From peer and teacher critiques of their product to suggested revisions for their business proposals, students obtain information about specific ways to improve their work, and their strengths are affirmed. Based on this feedback, they make changes to their work. To maximize the effectiveness of the critiques, continually model how to provide constructive criticism.

Public Products

As Larmer, Mergendoller, and Boss (2015) note, sharing student work with an outside audience increases student engagement, encourages students to do their best work, and provides authenticity.

Student reflections, as well as the products and presentations, corroborate their findings. Throughout the unit, students are engaged in learning and are motivated to produce quality products because of the outside audience—a panel of judges. You'll find business teams carefully reviewing their slide presentation for visual appeal and editing and revising texts multiple times without prompting. Moreover, their performance will improve as they implement changes their peers suggest. On the day of the presentations, have students dress professionally. Feedback on their performance will likely boost students' self-esteem as well.

Reference

Larmer, J., Mergendoller, J., & Boss, S. (2015). *Setting the standard for project-based learning: A proven approach to rigorous classroom instruction.* Alexandria, VA: ASCD.

Before You Start

Since securing a panel of judges to invest in the products is critical, consider sending out invitations six to eight weeks before the student presentations (Lesson 12). Invite people you know, parent volunteers, or people who come recommended. To increase students' motivation, you may want to ask your district superintendent or assistant superintendent to participate. Over time, we have also invited lawyers, businesspeople, and other community members to our panels. Make sure to have at least three but no more than five judges.

LESSON 1: Activator

Estimated Teaching Time: One 45-minute class period

Before You Start: Invite a marketing representative from a local company to your classroom to introduce the marketing process to students. If a marketing expert is not available, the following video clip explains how one idea became a reality: https://youtu.be/PpwIe6n3C-4

Materials

- *Shark Tank* video clip "Jack's Stand Pitch": https://youtu.be/i7jX9SR0bfw
- chart paper
- copies of Top Inventions Graphic Organizer (Reproducible 6A)
- classroom projection system
- computers or tablets with internet access
- guest speaker (see Before You Start, above)

Driving Question: How do we turn our ideas into inventions or innovations?

Critical Question: How do we begin to develop and market products?

Warm-Up: Explain to students that to explore how ideas become inventions and innovations, they will watch a *Shark*

(Available online; see page 7.)

Tank video clip of a young entrepreneur marketing his product. Ask them to pay attention to how the idea for the product emerged, why it was created, how it helps people, and what marketing strategies the entrepreneur used to convince the *Shark Tank* panel to invest in the product.

After watching the video, create an anchor chart on which to record students' observations. Write the following headings and have students add their thoughts under the appropriate heading:

- Why Created
- How It Helps
- Marketing Strategies

Tell students they will be working in teams to design or improve a product and pitch it to a panel of judges, similar to what happens in *Shark Tank*.

Teaching Steps

1. To spark students' creativity, distribute copies of Top Inventions Graphic Organizer. Direct students to use their devices and the QR code to access the article. (If necessary, demonstrate how to do this on the whiteboard.) Instruct students to choose one invention from each category, make an inference about how it changes someone's life, and record their thoughts on the organizer. Use gradual release (*I do, we do, you do*) to model inferencing before students work independently.

2. Divide the class into groups of four and have students share their responses within their groups.

3. Ask students which inventions they would purchase and why.

4. Explain to students the difference between an *invention* and an *innovation*. An invention is a product that has been created for the first time. It is based on an original idea. An innovation occurs when a person or group of people improve something that has already been invented.

5. Tell students that once an idea gives birth to an invention, the product needs to be marketed. Invite a marketing representative from a local company to introduce the marketing process to students and to do a real-life demonstration.

A marketing representative from Hershey Foods brought unmarked candy bars to our class and had students design ads to market the products.

Wrap-Up: With the class, create a flowchart that shows how products are marketed.

TIP To do a brief simulation of marketing a product, consider having the class set up a lemonade stand. Ask students: *What natural (things that occur naturally) and capital (human-made) resources will you need? What will you want in exchange for the product?*

LESSON 2: Teamwork and Problem-Solving

Estimated Teaching Time: One 45-minute class period

Before You Start: Effective teamwork is critical to the success of project-based learning. If possible, engage students in team-building activities, such as Saving Sam, Stranded on an Island, or Team Line, throughout the school year. (Instructions for these and other team-building activities are available online.) Before forming business teams for this unit, explicitly teach team-building skills and prepare anchor charts based on students' interactions and discussions. Have students reflect on skills they need to improve, then set a goal and form an action plan.

Materials

- chart paper
- markers
- plain paper
- pencils
- copies of Product Brainstorming (Reproducible 6B)
- small sentence strips

Driving Question: How do we turn our ideas into inventions or innovations?

Critical Question: How do we work effectively as a team?

Warm-Up: Divide the class into groups of 9 to 12 students. Have each group form a circle. Instruct them to join right hands with someone in the circle who is not next to them. Then, tell them to connect left hands with another person who is not next to them. Direct groups to untangle themselves without letting go of one another's hands. After the first group completes the task, have students return to their seats and discuss the following:

- What worked well?
- What problems did you encounter?
- What strategies can you use to solve these problems when we do the activity again?

Repeat the activity and discuss the differences students observed.

(Available online; see page 7.)

Students learn how to work as a team to untangle themselves.

Teaching Steps

1. Say to students: *Teamwork involves cooperating with one another to solve problems. Based on this activity and your experience working with groups, think about what teamwork looks like and sounds like.*

2. On a sheet of chart paper, write the title "What Teamwork Looks Like." As a whole class, discuss ideas and add them to the chart. Use the same process to create a second chart titled "What Teamwork Sounds Like." Display these charts in the classroom and refer to them as needed throughout the unit.

3. Form teams of three (see Tip). Distribute plain paper and pencils to each team. Have them brainstorm rules or procedures that are key to working together. Model two or three examples first (e.g., listen to one another, divide the work evenly, do your job). Circulate and monitor students' work.

> **TIP** To form business teams, group students according to their strengths. Try to include a writer, an organizer, and a technology-savvy student in each business team. Throughout the unit, students will use cooperative-learning rubrics to self- and peer-evaluate their ability to work as a team. On a daily basis, provide specific feedback to teams regarding these skills and work with them to solve problems among team members.

4. When teams finish brainstorming, distribute chart paper and markers. Have students title the paper "Rules for Teamwork." Tell them to decide on a minimum of five rules and take turns writing these rules on the paper.

5. Pair up teams and have them review each other's work, noting what they have in common. Encourage teams to "borrow" a rule from the other team and add it to their chart.

6. Collect teams' charts. (In the next lesson, you will return them to their respective teams, and students will refer to these rules regularly as they work on their products throughout this unit).

7. Tell students: *To work effectively as a team to create an invention or innovation, you need to come to the group with your ideas.* Distribute copies of Product Brainstorming and have students generate their own ideas for inventions. Tell them they will need these ideas to participate in tomorrow's lesson. (You can assign this as homework and proceed with the Wrap-Up.)

Wrap-Up: Distribute sentence strips to students. Ask them to reflect on how they interact with their peers when doing group work. Then, direct them to set one goal to improve their ability to work in a team. Model how to set a goal: *I will listen actively.* Encourage students to use strong action verbs when setting goals. After they write their goals on sentence strips, tell them to develop an action plan. Ask them what steps they should take to become active listeners and list these steps on the board. Students can then refer to the model as they create their own action plans and write them on their strips. Collect the strips from each team.

LESSON 3: Developing and Investigating a Product Idea

Estimated Teaching Time: One 45-minute class period

Before You Start: Prior to starting the unit, order 10-pocket organizers—folders with 10 inside pockets, including one inside the front and back covers—one for each team of three students. On the front cover of each business team's folder, list students' names. Inside the folders, create four tabs labeled "Business," "Product," "Letter," and "Presentation" to help students store and organize their materials (there are two pockets in each section). On the front-cover inside pocket, put a sticker labeled "Cooperative Rubrics," where students can store these evaluations of their soft skills, track their progress, and set new goals based on the scores. Place each team's goal-setting sentence strips (from Lesson 2) in this pocket. Place each team's "Rules for Teamwork" chart (also from Lesson 2) in the Business section of their folder.

At the start of each lesson, have teams place their business folders on their desks. Each reproducible you distribute will be labeled with one of the following abbreviations so that students will know in which pocket to put each handout:

C = Cooperative Rubrics
B = Business
PROD = Product
L = Letter
PRES = Presentation

Sample business folder

Materials
- seating chart (see Warm-Up)
- teams' business folders (see Before You Start)
- students' completed Product Brainstorming – PROD (from Lesson 2)
- copies of Investigating Our Idea – PROD (Reproducible 6C)
- computers or tablets with internet access
- writer's notebooks

Driving Question: How do we turn our ideas into inventions or innovations?

Critical Questions:
- How do we use our ideas to develop a product?
- How do we investigate whether our idea is original or already exists?

Warm-Up: Create a seating chart to place students with their business teams. Distribute the business folders. Direct students to take out their "Rules for Teamwork" chart and read the rules they agreed upon. Then have each member share his or her goal and action plan for becoming a team player.

(Available online; see page 7.)

Teaching Steps

1. Tell students to place their completed Product Brainstorming sheet on their desk. Instruct them to take turns sharing their product ideas with their team. As they listen to their teammates, ask students to think about the product ideas. Are they realistic? Is it possible to create them? Does something like it already exist?

2. Afterward, write the word *compromise* on the board. Ask students: *What does this word mean?* (to accept something that is not exactly what you wanted in order to come to an agreement) Encourage them to think about how to combine their collective ideas and compromise to create their invention or innovation. For example, if one student's idea is to create blinds that automatically close when someone looks in the window, and another student in the team has designed a sensor, the team can combine those ideas and use the sensor to detect a person peering into the house.

Sample Product Brainstorming sheet

3. Direct teams to choose one idea for their product. This choice can come from an individual's brainstorming sheet, from merging ideas, or from a new idea inspired by the team's discussion.

4. Distribute to each team a copy of Investigating Our Idea. Have teams search the internet for products that are similar to theirs to determine whether they have truly created an invention or have created an innovation. Tell them to record the prices of similar products as well. Remind students that if they discover their product idea is not original, they will need to revise it and research the new idea. Additionally, have students investigate the costs for materials and parts needed to create their invention or innovation. For example, if a team needs a spring or a sensor for their product, they must research its cost.

Wrap-Up: Distribute writer's notebooks. On a blank page, have students write the title "Reflections on Sharing Product Ideas." Next, ask them to take out their own goal statement from their business folder and to reflect on what they did during the team discussion that helped them meet their goal. Direct them to note other improvements they need to make to function effectively within the team. Write the following questions on the board and have students respond to them:

- What role did you play in your business team? Were you a leader, contributor, nonparticipant, or problem solver? Justify your response.
- Briefly describe the process your business team used to choose your idea. Did you choose an idea that someone brought to the team? Did you compromise? Did you come up with a new idea?

TIP In this lesson, one problem you might run into relates to the decision-making process and compromising on an idea. In our experience, we have had students who are completely committed to their idea and refused to make changes to their original invention/innovation. In most cases, we could jump in as mediators and provide new ways to combine ideas. However, in some cases, disputes continued when it was time to make the final decision. In these situations, we had each team member choose his or her favorite aspect of the invention. Then we integrated these into a single creation. In addition, we also have had difficulties when a strong-willed member of the team was absent and was upset that he or she did not have input into the decision-making process. Attempting to integrate the absentee's ideas into the final product usually alleviated this problem.

LESSON 4: Planning the Invention or Innovation

Estimated Teaching Time: One 45-minute class period

Materials

- teams' business folders
- teams' completed Investigating Our Idea (from Lesson 3)
- copies of the Invention Planner – PROD (Reproducible 6D)
- copies of the Cooperative Rubric: Product Planning – C (Reproducible 6E)

Driving Question: How do we turn our ideas into inventions or innovations?

Critical Question: How do we use our ideas to develop a product?

Warm-Up: Distribute business folders to the teams. Instruct students to take out their completed Investigating Our Idea handout. Ask them to review their product idea and to make changes based on what they discovered through their research.

Teaching Steps

1. Say: *Now that you have investigated your product idea and determined that it is original, you will need to plan for its development.* Give each team a copy of the Invention Planner. Explain that the teams need to do the following and record the information on their planners:

   - Choose a product name.
   - Describe what the product is.
   - Explain how the product works.
   - Explain how the product will change or improve a person's life.

2. Next, direct students to draw a sketch of the product on the back of the planner and to label the parts of the product.

3. Explain that each team will build a physical model of the product they sketched. Invite them to brainstorm ideas for the materials they will use to construct the product. Emphasize that they can use ordinary materials they have at home; they do not need to purchase items. Once the team decides on the materials, have each member

(Available online; see page 7.)

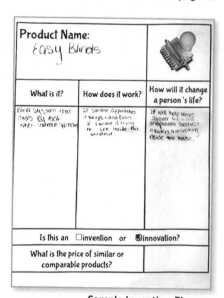

Sample Invention Planner

> **TIP** Some teams may disagree over the name of a product. Since soft skills can make or break a career, we truly believe such disputes are important for students to experience and learn from at a young age. For this reason, we ask students to reflect on how they work together.

write down what he or she will contribute. Set a specific date for bringing the materials to class and prepare a storage area to house them.

Wrap-Up: Give a copy of Cooperative Rubric: Product Planning to each student. Explain that students will independently rate themselves and their team members on their teamwork skills. Tell them to complete the sentence stems to justify their ratings. A sentence stem will be blank if a team member does not meet the criterion or needs improvement. Additional comments include compliments about superior work or suggestions for improvement. The team will evaluate the overall quality of the work together.

After students complete their individual evaluations, direct them to take turns discussing their ratings with their team. Afterward, tell students to set a realistic goal for the next team activity. Model examples and non-examples of effective goals before students write theirs. An example of an effective goal is: *We will appoint a group taskmaster to remind each person in the group to stay on task.* A non-example is: *We will try to do a better job of staying on task.* Provide time for team members to share their goals. Collect the rubrics and review them to monitor each team's progress and to determine what interventions, if any, are needed.

LESSON 5: Creating a Survey

Estimated Teaching Time: One 45-minute class period, plus a few days to collect data

Materials
- teams' business folders
- sticky notes
- letter-size paper copies and ledger-size card-stock copies of the Product Viability Survey – PROD (Reproducible 6F)
- classroom projection system
- teams' completed Invention Planners (from Lesson 4)
- copies of Sample Survey Form – PROD (Reproducible 6G)
- colored pencils and markers
- students' completed Cooperative Rubric: Product Planning (from Lesson 4)
- copies of Self-Assessment: Survey Poster – C (Reproducible 6H)

Driving Question: How do we turn our ideas into inventions or innovations?

Critical Question: How do we know if our product is viable?

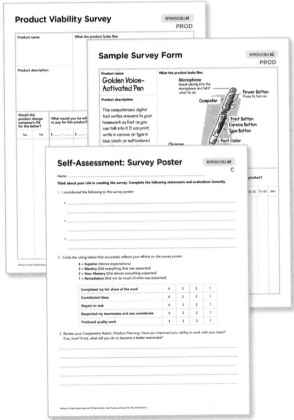

(Available online; see page 7.)

Warm-Up: Put students in their business teams. Distribute sticky notes to each student. Display a copy of the Product Viability Survey onto the whiteboard. Explain that *viability* means "capable of working or succeeding." Ask students what they observe about the survey planner. Direct them to record their observations on sticky notes. Have team members share their observations with one another. As a class, discuss what information will be gleaned from the survey and why the business teams need to know it.

Teaching Steps

1. Distribute to each team a letter-size copy of the Product Viability Survey. Tell students to do the following on the survey planner:

   - Fill out the name of their invention.
   - Draw a picture of what their invention looks like and label its parts. (Remind students to use the sketch they made on their Invention Planners to help them.)
   - Write a brief description of their product.
   - Fill in the price range and decide on an age group for the product.

2. Direct team members to divide the labor: One student can draw, while the other two draft the description and complete the information at the bottom of the planner. Give each team a copy of the Sample Survey Form to use as an example to guide their work.

3. Return the Cooperative Rubric: Product Planning to each team. Tell students to review the goals that they set for improving their ability to work well with others. Remind them to try to attain the teamwork goal they set during the previous lesson.

4. Pair up teams to critique and review each other's survey planners. After students revise their Product Viability Survey, give each team a card-stock copy of the survey to complete.

5. Hang the card-stock surveys in the school cafeteria or another public forum where teachers are available to monitor. Allow two days for other classes and students to put their tally marks on the posters.

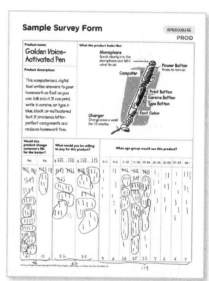

Sample survey

Wrap-Up: Distribute a copy of the Self-Assessment: Survey Poster to each student. Review the directions and provide time for students to complete it. Have team members share their responses to question 3 and provide additional feedback about positive changes and areas to improve.

TIP Since students' tally marks can be inconsistent and hard to decipher on handwritten surveys, consider conducting the product survey through Google Forms. You may even be able to share the forms with other schools in your district, to add validity to the data collection.

LESSON 6: Creating the Business Names and Logos

Estimated Teaching Time: One 45-minute class period

Materials

- dry-erase whiteboards and markers
- computers or tablets with internet access
- teams' business folders
- copies of Brainstorming a Business Name and Logo – B (Reproducible 6I)
- classroom projection system
- Guess the Logo quiz: https://bit.ly/355S1YE
- copies of Evaluating Group Progress: Business Name and Logo – B (Reproducible 6J)
- copy paper
- coloring supplies

Driving Question: How do we turn our ideas into inventions or innovations?

Critical Question: How do we promote our business?

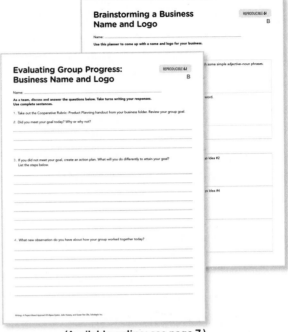

(Available online; see page 7.)

Warm-Up: Hand each team a dry-erase whiteboard and marker. Tell students: *Today, we're going to create our business cards. But first, we need to see what we know about business names. In your business teams, list as many business and company names as you can on a dry-erase board. When I call time, cap your markers.* After about two minutes, call time. Invite a team to name a business or company. If another team has the same company name, have them cross it out from their list so they do not repeat the same information when they share. Afterward, have the teams discuss why we might know these company names.

Teaching Steps

1. Ask students: *What do you think makes a company name memorable?* Discuss how a good company name is usually short and simple, easy to remember, and gives customers an idea of the company's products and services.

2. Give each student a copy of Brainstorming a Business Name and Logo. Have students complete the first four boxes of the organizer on their own.

3. After students finish, have them meet in their business teams to share their ideas. Tell teams their mission is to compromise on a name for their business.

4. Once all teams have chosen their business names, ask students: *What is the purpose of a logo?* Explain that a logo is a visual symbol that identifies a company.

> **TIP**
> As with all the URLs in this book, be sure to check the website before showing it to students. Some of the logos may not be appropriate for younger grades.

Display the Guess the Logo quiz (URL in Materials) on the whiteboard and challenge students to identify the different logos.

Sample business card

5. Afterward, instruct students to design some logos on their Brainstorming a Business Name and Logo sheets. Once students have at least one idea, have the business teams meet up again to accomplish their second mission of the day: designing a business logo for their company.

6. While students work together, look for teams that need assistance with coming to an agreement or even creating an idea. As teams complete their logos, pass out copy paper for the business teams to design a prototype for their business cards with the company name and logo.

> **TIP** The Avery website (www.avery.com/software/design-and-print) allows users to design business cards. You can take pictures of the logos and upload them to the cards. During the presentations (Lesson 12), students can hand their business cards to the judges.

Wrap-Up: Have each team introduce their company and logo by displaying their business card prototype. Invite students to give "stars and wishes" to the companies. ("Stars" are positive comments about what they like about the company name and logo, while "wishes" are suggestions for improvement.) After teams finish sharing their names and logos, distribute a copy of Evaluating Group Progress: Business Name and Logo to each team. Instruct teams to discuss the questions and to take turns writing their responses. Collect their reflection sheets afterward. Use the information to intervene where necessary or to determine if there's anything that needs to be discussed with a business team.

LESSON 7: Analyzing the Surveys

Estimated Teaching Time: One 45-minute class period

Materials

- computers or tablets with internet access
- classroom projection system
- teams' completed Product Viability Surveys (from Lesson 5)
- copies of Life Impact Survey Results Graph – PROD (Reproducible 6K)
- copies of Product Price Survey Results Graph – PROD (Reproducible 6L)

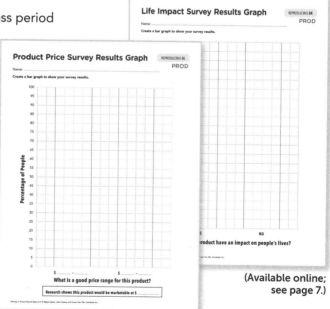

(Available online; see page 7.)

- copies of Target Audience Survey Results Graph – PROD
  (Reproducible 6M)
- copies of Group Assessment: Survey Analysis – C
  (Reproducible 6N)
- sticky notes

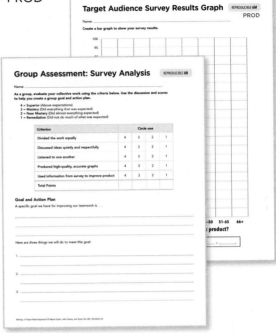

Driving Question: How do we turn our ideas into inventions or innovations?

Critical Question: How do we analyze surveys and use the results to market our products?

Warm-Up: Do an online image search for "product survey bar graph" and choose one to display on the whiteboard. (For example, a bar graph displaying people's enjoyment of different candy types, such as hard candy, licorice, jelly beans, and so on.) Pair up students and ask partners to read the bar graph and discuss what the results mean. Invite students to share their findings and discuss how companies use graphs to market their products.

(Available online; see page 7.)

Teaching Steps

1. Return each team's completed Product Viability Survey and give each team a copy of the Life Impact Survey Results Graph. Select one business team's Product Viability Survey to model step-by-step how to analyze the data for the Life Impact Survey Results Graph:

   a. Tally the yeses and noes.

   b. Count the total number of responses for the yeses and noes.

   c. Divide the number of yeses by the total number of responses, then multiply by 100 to arrive at the percentage.

   d. Divide the number of noes by the total number of responses, then multiply by 100.

   After each step, stop and allow teams time to do the calculations.

2. After students perform the calculations, ask them: *Based on the percentages, will this product change someone's life for the better? If not, how will you change your product?*

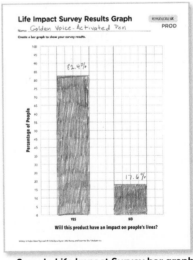

3. Using information from the team's survey used in step 1, model how to create a bar graph from the calculations. Color in the number of yeses in one color and the number of noes in a different color. Above each bar, write the percentages calculated.

Sample Life Impact Survey bar graph

4. Next, distribute to the teams copies of the Product Price Survey Results Graph. Choose a different team's Product Viability Survey and use the information on it to demonstrate how to construct the graph:

   a. Count the tally marks for the first price range.
   b. Divide the number by the total number of responses, then multiply by 100 to arrive at the percentage.
   c. Repeat steps a and b for the second price range.
   d. Use two different colors to create the bar graphs for the two price ranges and list the percentages above each one.

   Based on the results and the price calculated from the survey, ask students to determine the price range to sell the product.

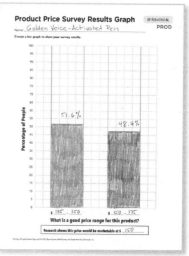

Sample Product Price Survey bar graph

5. Finally, give each team a copy of the Target Audience Survey Results Graph. Using another team's survey as a model, repeat the process outlined in step 4 to determine the age range for the product's target audience. This time, students will create nine color-coded bars, one for each age range. After the teams have completed their bar graphs, have them answer the following questions:

   • Based on your results, what age range will you target?
   • What happens to your product's viability if you have a broad age range?
   • If your age range is too narrow, what changes will you make to your product?

Wrap-Up: Pair up two teams. Have them exchange their bar graphs with each other and review them for accuracy. Also, instruct reviewers to make a list of changes or additions that need to be made to the bar graphs. Finally, have reviewers suggest one or two changes to the product that the survey indicates could enhance its success.

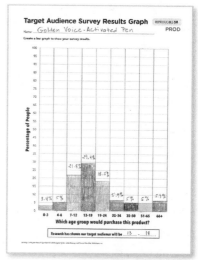

Sample Target Audience Survey bar graph

   Distribute copies of the Group Assessment: Survey Analysis to business teams. Model how to set a specific goal for improving teamwork and how to develop an action plan. For example, if a team's goal is to divide the work equally, the team's action plan could be to divide the work into manageable parts, assign one part to each team member, and help the others if someone finishes early.

TIP To stress the importance of using survey results to change a product idea, compare the process to revising a rough draft. Just as our peers make suggestions to help us improve our writing, the surveys show us what we need to fix to improve our invention. Through this discussion, students will begin to understand the value of interpreting the survey results and using them to create a better product.

LESSON 8: Building, Critiquing, and Revising Product Models

Estimated Teaching Time: Two 45-minute class periods

Before You Start: Prior to this lesson, ask students to bring in the materials and supplies they need to build their invention/innovation (see Lesson 4). Again, emphasize that they don't need to buy materials. Encourage them to look for things they can use at home.

Materials

- teams' business folders
- students' completed Invention Planner (from Lesson 4)
- materials and supplies for building the products
- copies of Building Checklist – PROD (Reproducible 6O)
- index cards, tape, scissors, writing tools
- copies of Product Critique – PROD (Reproducible 6P)
- copies of Cooperative Rubric: Building Product – C (Reproducible 6Q)

Driving Question: How do we turn our ideas into inventions or innovations?

Critical Question: How do we create a model of our product and improve it based on feedback?

Warm-Up: Have students take out their Invention Planners from their business folders. Tell them to review and, based on the feedback they've received so far, revise their description,

(Available online; see page 7.)

information about how the product works, and their assessment of how it will change a person's life. As they examine their sketches, ask them to consider what else needs to be added or changed.

Teaching Steps

1. Give each team a facedown copy of the Building Checklist. Before teams turn it over, direct members to number themselves from 1 to 3. Tell member #2, the Taskmaster, to take the checklist, assign and explain each member's roles, and move the team through the task.

   Note: The Gopher retrieves the materials the group brought to class, along with index cards, tape, and other supplies.

2. Allow time for the teams to construct their models.

3. Circulate and monitor the teams as they work. Take notes on members' interactions and use those notes to provide specific feedback to each team.

4. After teams complete their models, distribute to each team a copy of the Product Critique. Tell teams to fill out the information at the top.

5. Pair up two teams and have them take turns sharing their product. After one team presents, tell the other team to complete a critique sheet and provide oral feedback on the model, noting two strengths and two areas to improve. For example, reviewers may note that a device is too complex and does too many tasks. Maybe they are not sure how the device works and need a more detailed description of it.

6. Provide time for teams to improve their models.

Wrap-Up: Distribute copies of the Cooperative Rubric: Building Product. Instruct teams to complete the rubric. Afterward, invite teams to share some of the problems they faced and how they solved them.

Working together to build their invention

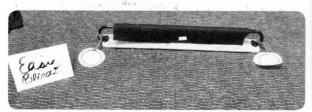
Finished product

LESSON 9: Writing, Revising, and Critiquing the Business Proposal

Estimated Teaching Time: Four 45-minute class periods

Four-Day Overview
- Day 1: Students review the model business proposal, plan the body paragraphs of their letter, and draft them.
- Day 2: Since everyone in the team writes one body paragraph, the team confers and revises their body paragraphs for consistency. Additionally, team members review the introduction and conclusion of the model letter and then collectively draft their own.
- Day 3: Team members type their drafts on Google Docs as a shared document.
- Day 4: Students revise and edit.

Before You Start: On Google Drive, create a document for each business team to access when they begin typing their business proposal.

Materials

- copies of the Model Business Proposal – L (Reproducible 6R)
- computers or tablets with internet access
- stapled and collated copies of the Business Proposal Assignment Packet – L (Reproducible 6S)
- copies of the Business Proposal Rubric – L (Reproducible 6T)
- classroom projection system
- copies of Revision Checklist: Business Proposal – L (Reproducible 6U)
- copies of Peer Conferencing Sheet for Business Proposal – L (Reproducible 6V)
- writer's notebooks

Driving Question: How do we turn our ideas into inventions or innovations?

Critical Question: How do we write a business proposal?

Warm-Up: Display the Model Business Proposal on the whiteboard. Draw students' attention to the letter's format, noting the sender's address, date, inside address, salutation, signature, and other features. Tell students to listen carefully as you read the letter aloud to determine its purpose and to think about what the writers do to achieve that purpose. After reading the Model Business Proposal, pair up students and have partners take turns identifying the writer's purpose and discussing how it is achieved. Then, invite students to share responses with the class.

Next, distribute copies of the model letter. Ask students to read paragraph one carefully, thinking about what it does and why. Tell students to write their responses in the margins. Afterward, discuss students' ideas. In addition, ask them to identify words or phrases that convince the audience that the company is successful and employs top-notch people. Continue this process of carefully examining each paragraph, explaining what it does and why, and identifying keywords and phrases.

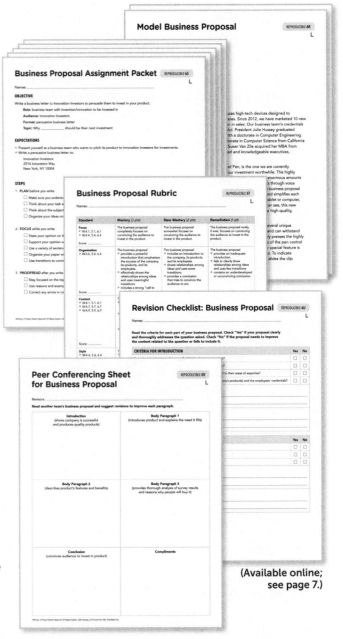

(Available online; see page 7.)

Teaching Steps

1. Put students in their business teams. Hand out to business teams copies of the Business Proposal Assignment Packet and Business Proposal Rubric and review their content.

2. Instruct team members to work together to complete the Business Proposal Thought Sheet (part of the packet), making sure that each member writes two sections of the planner.

3. When students complete the prewriting, have them look at the Business Letter Format and use it for reference as they draft their proposal, using the Letter Drafting Sheets (also in the packet). Explain that each team member is responsible for writing one body paragraph. Allow team members to choose which paragraph to write and give that member the appropriate drafting page. Monitor the teams as students write.

4. After team members finish drafting their paragraphs, have each student read his or her paragraph aloud to the team. Instruct listeners to jot down any questions, comments, or suggestions they have for the writer. Use a student volunteer to model this process before teams begin working.

5. Have students look at the Model Business Proposal again and read the introduction aloud. Using the model as a guide, ask students: *What specifically does the introduction of the letter need to include?* Through questioning, elicit the following information and write it on the board:

   - The name of the company
   - What the company does
   - A notable fact about the company's success (name a few of the products, refer to money from sales, and so on)
   - Credentials for the members of the company

6. Explain that even though students will need to "invent" some of the information for this paragraph, what they write should sound as realistic as possible. That means they may have to research some of the colleges, universities, and degrees that illustrate the team members' expertise. Note that their credentials should be related to the product they are marketing. For example, if they are marketing a robot, they need to identify a university that is known for computer engineering, such as MIT.

7. Tell students that the whole team will write the introduction. One person will write while the other two contribute ideas. Provide time for students to draft the introduction.

8. Follow a similar process for the conclusion. Emphasize that students need to include the amount of money they want investors to contribute for a percentage of their company. Also, note that students should include in this closing paragraph persuasive techniques and powerful facts about the success of their product.

9. After teams have completed their drafts, have members type their paragraphs into the Google Doc stored in Google Drive. Instruct each team member to type his or her own body paragraph. Whoever finishes first can begin typing the introduction. Another team member can type the conclusion, while the third member reviews the typed paragraphs and makes comments.

10. Give each team a copy of the Revision Checklist: Business Proposal to review the content of each paragraph and to make other revisions on their draft. Instruct teams to print their documents when they finish.

11. Distribute to each team a copy of the Peer Conferencing Sheet for Business Proposal. Tell students to place the printed copy of their business proposal next to it.

12. Explain that each team will read another team's proposal, paragraph-by-paragraph. After reading each paragraph, reviewers should write in the appropriate box specific suggestions for revision. Using a business team's letter, read the introduction aloud and model effective suggestions for revision. Write these on the board. Using a different team's letter, read the first body paragraph aloud and repeat the process. If necessary, continue modeling until the class has a clear understanding of how to proceed. See below for examples of effective comments.

> **TIP** Here's another revision strategy teams can use: Pair up students from two different business teams and have them sit back-to-back. As one student reads the product description, the other draws the product. Whatever is missing in the drawing should be included in the written description.

Examples of Revisions

Revision Suggestions for the Introduction	**Revision Suggestions for Body Paragraph 1**
• Need to include what company does. • Show how the employees' credentials relate to the quality of the company's product. • Three sentences start with "Our company." How can you change some of your sentence beginnings? • Replace the weak verb *are* with a vivid verb.	• Why is your product better than others? Add this information to your paragraph. • Sentence 3 seems like a great topic sentence. Think about moving it. • Add a transition to sentence 5. We are not sure how it relates to sentence 4. • Where is the clincher?

13. Assign each business team another team's letter to revise. Have team members take turns writing suggestions for each paragraph. Then have each team rotate to another letter, repeating this process two or three times. This way, each team receives enough feedback to make meaningful revisions to their proposal while having the experience of reading other proposals. Time the rotations, allotting about 10 to 15 minutes each.

14. When students return to their seats, ask them to read the suggested revisions and highlight the ones they will implement. Have students open their Google Docs and revise the introduction together. Then, have each team member revise his or her own body paragraph. Together, the team can revise the conclusion.

15. After all revisions have been made, have each team reread their proposal, make remaining changes, and edit their paper.

Wrap-Up: Have students open to a blank page in their writer's notebooks and respond to the following questions:

- What problems did your team encounter when writing the business proposal?
- How did you resolve the problem? If the problem was not resolved, what could you do to resolve a similar problem in the future?
- Specifically, what did you contribute to the team?
- How can you strengthen your ability to work in teams?

LESSON 10: Planning, Producing, and Critiquing the Product Commercial

Estimated Teaching Time: Two 45-minute class periods

Materials

- links to student exemplar commercials:
  - https://youtu.be/H7kljAwPW1A
  - https://youtu.be/G8AZpRUiO3A
- computers or tablets with internet access
- classroom projection system
- chart paper
- markers
- construction paper
- Commercial Storyboard Planner – PRES (Reproducible 6W)
- devices for students to record commercials
- iMovie or similar video editor app
- copies of Cooperative Rubric: Commercial – C (Reproducible 6X)

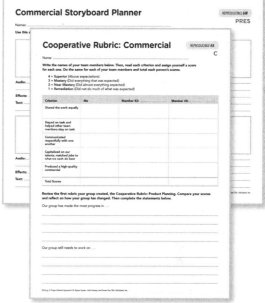

(Available online; see page 7.)

Driving Question: How do we turn our ideas into inventions or innovations?

Critical Question: What persuasive techniques can we use to enhance our commercial?

Warm-Up: As the class begins, play the student exemplar commercials (links above) on a whiteboard. Pause the videos and tell students to observe what makes these commercials effective (e.g., humor, a catchy slogan, emotional appeal). After the class has viewed both commercials, engage students in a discussion about what makes them memorable. Ask: *What is the purpose of each commercial? What is each one "selling"?* With the class, create an anchor chart about commercials— what's their purpose, what makes them effective and memorable, what information needs to be included, and so on.

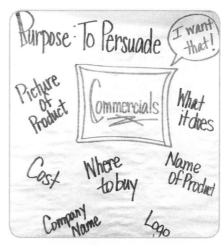

Create an anchor chart about what makes a commercial effective and memorable.

Teaching Steps

1. Have students meet with their business teams to brainstorm ideas about what their product commercial will do, contain, and portray. Remind them that commercials use persuasive techniques to promote products and convince consumers to buy them.

2. Give each team a sheet of construction paper and a marker. Have teams map out their vision in words, pictures, sketches, and/or symbols.

3. After they have sketched out their vision on paper, have each business team access the app they will use to create a commercial for their product. Allow them time to explore and decide on the format for their commercial.

4. When teams have made their decisions, distribute copies of the Commercial Storyboard Planner and have them begin filling it out.

5. As teams work, circulate around the room so students have access to you if they have difficulty compromising or developing an idea. Once they have laid out the storyboard for their commercial, have the business teams begin filming and piecing their commercial together.

TIP Using a planner helps students think about the details they need to include to make a quality commercial. Some students may be well versed in using video-making apps and resist using a planner. However, strongly encourage them to jot the words in the text boxes to accommodate team members' various learning styles.

6. When a business team claims to be finished, ask members to "test market" its commercial with another team for feedback. Teams should edit and revise their commercials based on feedback.

7. As business teams complete filming and editing their commercials, have them share the videos with you to upload to YouTube or your preferred sharing platform.

8. Hand out copies of Cooperative Rubric: Commercial. Instruct students to reflect on the commercial-making process and their group's ability to compromise and work as a team during the commercial creation.

Wrap-Up: As soon as business teams complete their commercials and cooperative rubrics, gather them for a class viewing of all the commercials. After watching each commercial, ask students to partner with a person seated next to them and to name the product, price, and company; state where to buy the product; and explain what the product does. Allow time for compliments and suggestions for improvement, too.

LESSON 11: Planning, Creating, Critiquing, and Rehearsing the Multimedia Presentation

Estimated Teaching Time: Two to three 45-minute class periods

Materials
- student multimedia presentation exemplar: https://youtu.be/cBuQnQK7Ol4
- computers or tablets with internet access
- classroom projection system
- copies of Product Presentation Planner Packet – PRES (Reproducible 6Y)

(Available online; see page 7.)

- copies of Product Presentation Rubric – PRES (Reproducible 6Z)
- Google Slides, PowerPoint, or another presentation platform (e.g., trifold board)
- index cards
- chart paper
- Presentation Good/Bad Examples video: https://youtu.be/S5c1susCPAE
- copies of the Slideshow Checklist – PRES (Reproducible 6AA)
- copies of Judge's Evaluation Sheet – PRES (Reproducible 6BB)
- copies of Self-Assessment: Product Presentation – C (Reproducible 6CC)

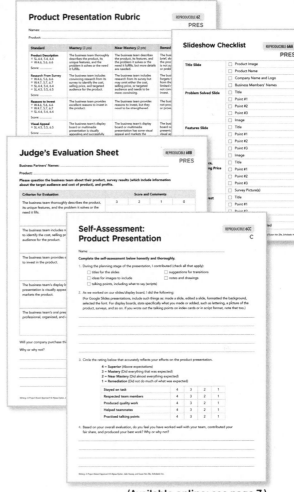

(Available online; see page 7.)

Driving Question: How do we turn our ideas into inventions or innovations?

Critical Question: How do we create and present an effective presentation?

Warm-Up: Address the driving question with students and review the process so far of creating an invention or innovation with the business teams:

- compromising on the product
- designing and analyzing surveys
- building a model of the product
- writing a business proposal
- developing a commercial

Announce that they're going to use all the materials they have generated to produce a multimedia presentation for the judges. To start, have the class watch the student exemplar presentation (link in Materials). Ask students to evaluate the presentation and discuss its strengths and weaknesses.

Teaching Steps

1. Give each team a copy of the Product Presentation Planner Packet and the Product Presentation Rubric. Have students review the packet and discuss expectations for the project.

2. Afterward, discuss the following questions with the class:

   - Does your commercial provide enough information for the judges to invest in your product? How can you maximize its effectiveness? (Need to embed our commercial into the slide presentation.)
   - How many slides must you have? (Five slides) Who creates them? (Each team member contributes equally.)
   - Who speaks during the presentation? How many times does each team member speak? (Each team member speaks an equal number of times.)

3. Allot time for the business teams to plan their presentations. Explain the importance of knowing what they want to say, who is going to say what, and how they are going to deliver the information. As they work, circulate and conference with each business team. Once a team has finished planning its presentation, review the rubric with them.

4. Provide time for business teams to create their product presentations—either on the computer or on a trifold board.

5. When business teams finish the draft for their presentation, distribute copies of the Slideshow Checklist to determine whether they have included all the elements and to make appropriate revisions.

6. Afterward, instruct each team member to write on an index card what he or she will say. Then, have the team practice their talking points while using their slide presentation or trifold board. Emphasize that students need to memorize their parts before the actual presentations.

> **TIPS** Google Slides allow students to create a document and share it with one another. Collaborating on the same document with different devices simultaneously saves time.
>
> Allow two class periods for teams to create their slide presentations. Use a third period to discuss public-speaking skills and allow teams to practice the presentations.

7. Call the class together and discuss the dos and don'ts of public speaking. Record their ideas on chart paper. As a class, view the Presentation Good/Bad Examples video online (URL in Materials). Then, ask students to add to the anchor chart new information they learned and to delete unnecessary information.

8. Remind students that they need to dress professionally for their presentations. Spend a few minutes discussing what "dressing professionally" means.

9. Advise students that practicing their presentations and speaking skills will help ease their jitters. Provide 25 to 30 minutes for teams to practice, practice, practice their presentations.

10. Invite one team to present to the class and videotape their performance. Show the video to the class. Display the Judge's Evaluation Sheet on the whiteboard. Remind students about the importance of constructive criticism, and then involve the class in evaluating the presentation.

> **TIP** "A picture is worth a thousand words." After a team models, videotapes, and watches their presentation, students often have a better understanding of what needs to be revised or even overhauled. Watching other presentations often helps teams realize the difference between an excellent presentation and a mediocre one. Then, they can use this knowledge to improve their own performances.

Wrap-Up: Pair up business teams and have them perform their presentation for each other. Briefly remind the teams about the importance of volume and projection. Give each team a copy of the Judge's Evaluation Sheet to complete as they watch their peers. After each presentation, have teams share their evaluation, ask for clarification if necessary, and make appropriate changes.

> **TIP** About a week before the actual student presentations, send a reminder to your panel of judges. Provide the date and time of the presentations, as well as the expected total length of time for all the presentations.

Distribute copies of Self-Assessment: Product Presentation and have students complete it. Collect these and use them to monitor students' progress with soft skills.

LESSON 12: Public Presentations and Final Reflections

Estimated Presentation Time: 10–15 minutes per presentation

Before You Start: If possible, prepare the room the night before the presentations. Set up a judge's table and create a nameplate for each judge. In front of each judge's seat, place each team's business proposal with their business card stapled to it along with a copy of the Judge's Evaluation Sheet. Stack the business proposals in the same order as the presentations. Load each team's multimedia presentation onto a computer, ready to be played.

Materials

- copies of each team's business proposal with their business card attached (one for each judge)
- copies of Judge's Evaluation Sheet – PRES (Reproducible 6BB)
- copies of Audience Note Sheet – PRES (Reproducible 6DD)
- copies of Final Reflection – C (Reproducible 6EE)
- classroom projection system
- microphones for presenters

Driving Question: How do we turn our ideas into inventions or innovations?

Critical Question: How do we effectively present our product ideas to a professional audience?

Warm-Up: Prior to the presentations, have business teams rehearse individually one final time and provide feedback to one another.

Presentation Steps

1. Greet the judges and review the Judge's Evaluation Sheet with them. Invite them to peruse the business proposals while business teams prepare for their presentations.

(Available online; see page 7.)

2. Introduce the judges. Distribute copies of the Audience Note Sheet to students. Explain that they will use these sheets to record information about each product and use that to determine which ones they think are worthy of their investment and why.

3. Begin the presentations. After each presentation, allow time for questions from the judges and audience.

4. After the final presentation, provide time for judges to make the decision about which product they will invest in.

5. While judges are deliberating, tell students to turn their notes over and write down the product they will invest in and why.

6. When the judges are ready, have them announce the winner and provide reasons why they will invest in the product.

Encourage students to dress professionally for their presentations.

Wrap-Up: After the judges have left, distribute copies of the Final Reflection sheet for students to complete. Compile their comments on chart paper or on a Google Doc projected on the whiteboard. Use students' input to revise the unit.

Invite outside judges to evaluate each team's presentation.

Final Thoughts

Why is implementing project-based learning so important? Consider the following student responses about the things they learned.

The things I learned:
- *How to work hard*
- *How to work together on something and achieve a goal*
- *How to make different products from combining ideas*
- *How to be an entrepreneur and create things from ideas*
- *Teamwork leads to success*

These comments prove that involving students in PBL teaches them the value of compromise, teamwork, goal-setting, and the process of turning an idea into a tangible product. PBL makes learning meaningful and relevant; students are doing what future employers need them to do.

Since we have begun using PBL in our classrooms, we have witnessed its positive impact on our students. Their excitement and enthusiasm for learning has soared, and the quality of their final products has improved significantly because students are invested in what they are doing. So, join us on our journey to inspire, motivate, and challenge students as we embrace the principles of PBL and strive to prepare our students to face the 21st century with joy.